INBOUND MARKETING

ATTRACT, ENGAGE, AND DELIGHT CUSTOMERS ONLINE

REVISED AND UPDATED
SECOND EDITION

BRIAN HALLIGAN

DHARMESH SHAH

WILEY

Contents

Foreword

We're living a revolution!

We're living an ongoing revolution in the way people communicate. How did a relatively unknown, young, single-term black senator with funny ears and a funnier name get elected President of the United States, not once but twice? Simple: He and his team understood the revolution and harnessed the power of the web to communicate effectively with the masses. They built an online following of tens of millions and raised half a billion dollars, much of it from small donations on the web.

We're living a revolution in the way people find products and choose companies to do business with. These days, practically everyone turns to the web first when researching anything—from the best baby stroller to buy to which corporate accounting firm to hire for your business. We start at Google or another search engine and we tap our online network of friends, family members, and colleagues via online tools like e-mail, instant messaging, Skype, Facebook, and Twitter.

We're living a revolution where the companies that attract our attention are not the ones with big budgets and glitzy TV ads. Now we pay attention to the ones with great web content, like Quark Expeditions, a polar travel outfitter that uses content people find via search engine to fill expedition ships while the competition relies on expensive advertising and direct mail. When I wanted to travel to Antarctica, I found Quark Expeditions online and booked my journey.

Clearly, a great web presence is critical for any business. Inbound marketing is at the forefront of the revolution.

And with revolution comes liberation!

We're liberated from the tyranny of marketing effectiveness being determined by the size of our wallets. Today, anyone with a story to tell can command an audience—and customers—on the web. Your potential customers are looking for products and services like yours right now, today, this minute.

We're liberated from the tyranny of having to interrupt people's daily lives to try to market to them. Rather than grasping for buyers' attention with expensive ad campaigns, now we can publish engaging and useful information on the web and deliver it exactly when people are interested. People land on our virtual doorstep. This is a dream come true!

We're liberated from the tyranny of always relying on mainstream media to get our information into the marketplace. Now we can tell our story directly. And the best part is that when you tell the story well, you'll get found by people who are eager to do business with you.

Inbound marketing is about getting found online, through search engines and on social networking sites that billions of people use to find answers each day.

We've come a long way since the first edition of *Inbound Marketing* was released in 2009. You'll read about updated strategies for success in these pages. The tools of inbound marketing are constantly evolving, and new ways to communicate have been launched such as Instagram, Foursquare, and Google+. Consider these remarkable stats: In 2009, Twitter had 18 million users, and now it has 241 million; Facebook has grown during the same time from 150 million mostly student users to 1.3 billion people around the world. Mobile has exploded in importance with 6.8 billion mobile phone subscriptions on a planet of 7 billion people! It's never been easier to reach buyers on the web.

While the strategies of inbound marketing are similar to those in the first edition of this book, Brian and Dharmesh have completely updated the tactics for our new environment.

Oh, and one more thing that's gotten better in the past five years: Marketing is more fun than ever! When was the last time you got excited about buying yet another contact list of people you could interrupt? Never, right? Creating content and engaging with buyers on social networks is empowering. Inbound marketing is fun, and with it comes a more rewarding way to live.

But as in every revolution, the rules have changed. If you're like me and you've grown up with a traditional marketing education that focused on the "four P's," then you've got to unlearn what you have learned. If you have an MBA, or you've trained on the job, then you've got to unlearn what you have learned. You need to forget what worked in the past, in the offline world, before the revolution. You need to pick up some new skills.

Fortunately, we've got Brian and Dharmesh to show us the way. These guys are marketing visionaries who have helped millions of people get found online. Really. Today, millions of people are being found more often than they used to be because of Brian and Dharmesh's incredibly popular tools and pioneering ideas, like HubSpot Website Grader. And now they've collected all their years of experience into this book.

In these pages, you'll find marketing strategy and wisdom. But even more important, you'll find hundreds of practical and accessible ideas, tools, and techniques that you can apply to your business right now. *Inbound Marketing* is written by experts steeped in the realities of successful marketing, not academics who talk up the latest theory.

The great thing about inbound marketing is that anyone can do it. Including you. *Especially* you. It doesn't require a lot of money, but it does require an investment of your time and creativity.

What are you waiting for?

Continue reading to join the revolution, become liberated, have fun, and get found by your customers!

—David Meerman Scott
Best-selling author of
The New Rules of Marketing & PR
www.WebInkNow.com
twitter.com/dmscott

Acknowledgments

We want to thank numerous people for their help on this book. Thank you to David Meerman Scott, who pushed us to write the book in the first place and helped shepherd us through the process.

Thank you to the good folks at John Wiley & Sons for backing us and helping us create a great document, and thank you to Dianna Huff of DH Communications, Inc., for helping us with the final edits.

Thank you to the fantastic people at HubSpot who we have the privilege of working with every day.

Thank you to those who inspired and helped us:

David Meerman Scott (webinknow.com)

Seth Godin (sethgodin.typepad.com)

Kirsten Waerstad (CreativeEarth.com)

Paul Gillin (paulgillin.com)

Chris Brogan (chrisbrogan.com)

Gail Goodman (constantcontact.com)

Jack Welch (welchway.com)

Ray Ozzie (www.microsoft.com)

Tom Friedman (thomaslfriedman.com)

Guy Kawasaki (blog.guykawasaki.com)

W. Chan Kim, Renée Mauborgne (blueoceanstrategy.com)

Larry Weber (w2groupinc.com)

Jim Cash (www.generalcatalyst.com)

Greg Strakosch (TechTarget.com)

Steve Jobs (www.apple.com)

Rand Fishkin (Moz.com)

Michael McDerment (FreshBooks.com)

Jason Fried (37signals.com)

Brian Solis (briansolis.com)

Paul Roetzer (www.pr2020.com)

Todd Defren (pr-squared.com)

Geoffrey Moore (geoffmoore.blogs.com)

Tim O'Reilly (oreilly.com)

John Battelle (battellemedia.com)

Charlene Li (http://www.charleneli.com/blog)

Josh Bernoff (blogs.forrester.com/groundswell)

Clayton Christensen (www.hbs.edu)

Joe Lassiter (www.hbs.edu)

Thomas Steenburgh (www.hbs.edu)

Andrew McAfee (www.mit.edu)

Arnoldo Hax (www.mit.edu)

Duncan Simester (www.mit.edu)

Ed Roberts (www.mit.edu)

Michael Cusumano (www.mit.edu)

Brian Clark (CopyBlogger.com)

John Jantsch (DuctTapeMarketing.com)

Avinash Kaushik (Kaushik.net)

Steve Krug (sensible.com)

Darren Rowse (ProBlogger.net)

Steve Rubel (MicroPersuasion.com)

Aaron Wall (SEOBook.com)

Andy Beal (MarketingPilgrim.com)

Introduction

Raise your hand if you know a business that would like more visitors to its website, more leads for its sales team—and more customers to fuel growth. Chances are your hand is up. We all know businesses that want to grow. There are *millions* of them. Since you're reading this book, chances are, your business is one of them.

Now, raise your hand if you love getting cold calls from eager salespeople during dinner. Or spam e-mails with irrelevant offers in your inbox. How about popup ads when you're trying to read an article on the Internet? No hands up? Didn't think so. And, as it turns out, most other people share your sentiment.

The problem is that there's a fundamental mismatch between how organizations are marketing and selling their offerings—and the way that people *actually* want to shop and buy. We all want to help our organizations grow, but nobody (including marketers) likes the way we are commonly marketed to.

The Story Behind a Startlingly Simple Observation

In 2004 (a decade ago!), the two of us met while we were both graduate students at the Massachusetts Institute of Technology (MIT).

After graduation, Brian was helping venture-backed startups with their marketing and sales strategies, when he noticed a problem. The "best practices" marketing and sales playbook he had successfully used for years at previous companies wasn't working that well. Not only were the practices far from the "best," they were fundamentally broken. Trade shows, e-mail blasts, and advertisements just weren't that effective anymore. People weren't responding to these interruptive tactics and had gotten really good at blocking them out.

Madison Avenue, We Have a Problem

Meanwhile, Dharmesh was still at MIT, working on his graduate thesis. Between classes, he started a blog on startups and entrepreneurship.

He creatively named it OnStartups.com. The blog gained mass adoption—and massive traffic, which surprised us both.

The two of us would meet regularly to talk about Brian's work, Dharmesh's classes—and startups. One topic especially interested us: Why was a tiny blog written by an MIT grad student with no budget able to get so much more traffic and interest than companies with professional marketing teams and big budgets? What was going on here? What was Dharmesh doing? Rather than interrupt people with advertisements or e-mails, Dharmesh was figuring out ways to pull in people from Google, other blogs, and social media sites. All for free. With many late nights and experimentation, he figured out how to "get found" by thousands of people on the web.

After many meetings, much coffee, and the occasional wine or Belgian beer (a favorite for both of us), we came to a startlingly simple observation.

People did not want to be interrupted by marketers or harassed by salespeople. They wanted to be helped.

The world has changed dramatically: People no longer live, work, shop, and buy as they did a decade or two ago. And yet, businesses still try to market and sell like it's the 1990s.

Inbound: A More Effective Way to Attract, Engage, and Delight

Nothing is more powerful than an idea whose time has come.

—Victor Hugo

We started talking about this transformation in how people shop and buy. We called the traditional, interruptive methods "outbound marketing," because they were fundamentally about pushing a message out, and started calling the *new* way "inbound marketing." Inbound was about *pulling* people in by sharing relevant information, creating useful content, and generally being *helpful*.

So, we talked about this transformation to anyone who would listen—one-on-one meetings with local businesses in Boston, onstage at conferences with hundreds of people, and on our blog with thousands of readers. The response was overwhelmingly positive and incredibly exciting.

Inbound Was an Idea Whose Time Had Come

It is a fantastic time to be a marketer or an entrepreneur today. For the last 50 years, companies such as Procter & Gamble, IBM, and Coca-Cola used huge amounts of money to interrupt their way into businesses and consumers' wallets using outbound marketing techniques. The outbound marketing era is over. The next 50 years will be the era of inbound marketing.

Getting Businesses Off the Sidelines and Into the Game

The next question was, if the concept of inbound was so easy to understand and inspiring, why weren't more companies doing it? Why were millions of companies sitting on the sidelines instead of tapping into the power of this transformation?

The reason was clear: Though the idea of inbound made sense, people weren't completely sure how to get started and how to make it work for their business.

The problem wasn't a lack of tools. There were content management systems and SEO tools and social media applications and e-mail tools and marketing automation tools and on . . . and on . . . and on. Many of these individual tools were great—but the task of combining them was gargantuan. It wasn't within the realm of mere mortals who didn't command an impressive army of IT folks.

So, on June 9, 2006 (MIT commencement day), we officially started HubSpot—a software company based in Cambridge, Massachusetts. We started the company for two reasons. First, we believed in the transformative power of inbound marketing and how it could help businesses grow. Second, we wanted to make it easy for organizations to get into the game so we committed to building a platform *from the ground up* that was expressly designed to help them do it.

We built HubSpot with one simple goal: Make it easier to get going with inbound, so businesses could get growing. One platform to learn. One password to remember. One bill to pay. And, one phone number to call. One integrated system, designed from the ground up to transform how organizations market and sell.

Inbound Helped HubSpot Grow Spectacularly

We took all our ideas about how to market in this new way, and tried them at HubSpot. We started a blog, we produced videos, we did webinars, we wrote eBooks—we even started HubSpot Academy, which trains and certifies people on inbound marketing. Over 100,000 certifications have now been completed.

HubSpot now employs over 800 people and has 12,000 customers in over 70 countries across the globe. We attribute much of our success to inbound marketing, both applying it to our business and helping our customers apply it to theirs.

You Hold Our Secrets in Your Hands . . .

What you are now holding in your hands is the collective learnings we have had. The concepts of inbound marketing that we've learned and applied to HubSpot, and insights from thousands of companies that have seen the power of this new model work in their own companies.

Eight years ago, when we started HubSpot in a tiny one-room office a block away from the MIT campus, we thought we were starting a software company. We were wrong. We had not just started a software company, we had sparked an entire movement. The inbound movement now extends well beyond our four walls—it touches and transforms millions of individuals from all over the world.

We believe we're still in the early stages of the inbound movement, and the best is yet to come.

Thanks for joining us on this journey.

Brian Halligan (@bhalligan)
Dharmesh Shah (@dharmesh)

INBOUND MARKETING

Part I

Inbound Marketing

What gets us into trouble is not what we don't know. It's what we know for sure that just ain't so.

—*Mark Twain*

Chapter 1

Shopping Has Changed . . . Has Your Marketing?

The fundamental task of marketers is to spread the word about their products and services in order to get people to buy them. To accomplish this task, marketers use a combination of outbound techniques including e-mail blasts, telemarketing, direct mail, TV, radio, and print advertising, and trade shows (or expos) in order to reach their potential buyers. The problem with these traditional marketing techniques is that they have become less effective at spreading the word as people get better at blocking out these interruptions.

THE DIFFERENCE BETWEEN DIRECT MAIL AND JUNK MAIL

DIRECT MAIL IS WHAT YOU SEND AS A MARKETER. JUNK MAIL IS WHAT YOU RECEIVE AS A CONSUMER.

Twenty years ago, buying a large e-mail list of "targeted names" and sending newsletters and offers to addresses on this list worked well. Internet users now routinely employ spam filters, and the National

Canned Spam Act limits a marketer's ability to send "unsolicited messages" to people with whom the company does not have a relationship. According to the research firm MarketingSherpa, the average open rate for an e-mail blast has gone down from 39 percent in 2004 to less than 25 percent in 2014.

Twenty years ago, hiring your own internal sales force or contracting with an external telemarketing firm worked well. Then, Caller ID became a standard feature on home, work, and cell phones, and increasing numbers of people are signing up for the national Do Not Call Registry. A well-trained telesales rep can go a full day without having a decent conversation with a prospect.

Twenty years ago, sending a piece of direct mail to a large list of people was an effective way to get business because people often opened their mail. Today, mailboxes are full of junk mixed in with a few bills, so people pay less attention to them. Other than my grandmother, I don't know anyone who actually looks forward to sifting through their mail.

Twenty years ago, spending tens or hundreds of thousands of dollars on a TV advertisement was a guaranteed way to reach a large audience. More recently, people use TiVo/DVRs to skip advertisements. Further, the explosion of available TV channels and the rise of great video content online makes it difficult for advertisers to capture attention. Some of today's most popular shows (like Netflix's *House of Cards*) are free of advertising. This is not a small trend.

Twenty years ago, radio ads were heard by people in their cars, homes, and workplaces. Today, the emergence of XM/Sirius radio and music services like Pandora and Spotify has dramatically lowered advertising's reach, and the emergence of the iPod and iTunes has dramatically lowered the amount of radio people listen to at home and at work.

Twenty years ago, a trade show or conference was a surefire way for businesses to reach their target audience. Today, many trade shows have either gone out of business or have seen a significant decline. Only the very best and biggest events are able to draw significant attendees because people prefer to not spend money on flights, hotel costs, and so on. Many people visiting trade shows now are job seekers and other vendors—not buyers.

OVERCOMING TRADESHOW DEPRESSION

WITH NO PROSPECTS VISITING THEIR BOOTHS, JOE AND SUE GIVE EACH OTHER MORAL SUPPORT.

Twenty years ago, the trade publication was subscribed to and carefully read by most of your marketplace. Today, many trade publications have been losing subscribers and laying off staff. These highly qualified people are now starting their own blogs—some of which have become more popular than the publication they used to work for.

The bottom line is that people are sick and tired of being interrupted with traditional outbound marketing messages and have become quite adept at blocking marketers out.

Who Moved My Customers?

People shop and learn in a whole new way compared to just a few years ago, so marketers need to adapt or risk extinction. People now use the Internet to shop and gather information, but where on the Internet do they go—and how do they use the Internet for these activities? We can break the Internet down into three main areas.

People primarily shop and gather information through search engines, such as Google. The average information seeker conducts dozens of searches per day—and, rather than listen to a sales rep, read a spam message, watch a TV ad, or fly to a trade show, most people find it easier to sit at their desks and find the information online through Google. In order to take advantage of this new reality, marketers need to change the way they think about marketing— from the ground up.

Another place people gather information is the blogosphere and its more than 150 million blogs (as of this writing). Virtually every industry and consumer niche you can think of has a cadre of online pontificators, many of whom are quite good. Your target audience is no longer reading the trade publication, and instead is searching Google and subscribing to blogs written by the folks who used to write for the trade journal.

The third place people learn/shop is social media sites such as Twitter, Facebook, LinkedIn, Reddit, YouTube, and others.

To be successful and grow your organization, you need to match the way you market your products to the way your prospects learn about and shop for your products. And you do that by generating leads through inbound marketing.

Inbound in Action: Barack Obama for President

Regardless of your political views, you can apply the marketing principles Barack Obama used in his 2008 presidential campaign—a brilliant example of how to effectively use inbound marketing to beat bigger, better-funded rivals.

In the run up to the first campaign, Barack Obama was a little-known first-term senator from Illinois up against a well-known, well-funded Hillary Clinton political machine. Early in the race, Obama realized that using the same outbound marketing rules that Hillary would likely use would put him on the same playing field—*but the field would be tilted her way.*

Because he initially had less funding, Obama couldn't compete with Hillary and her e-mail blasts, telemarketing, direct mail campaigns, and TV and radio advertising. Instead of playing by the old rules, he made different rules altogether—many of which relied heavily on inbound marketing. "The aim of our online campaign," says Chris Hughes, cofounder of Facebook and Obama's Internet strategist, "was to help individuals understand the values of Barack Obama and of our campaign and then to make it as easy as possible for them to actively engage with the campaign's work. We tried to open as many direct channels of communication as possible—using e-mail, text messages, online networks—and then equip them with the tools to spread the campaign's message using networking technology such as My.BarackObama.com and Facebook."

The strategy worked. Americans were able to connect with Obama via his blog, Facebook page (5,800,000 supporters and counting), Twitter (450,000 followers and counting), LinkedIn (13,000 members and counting), and YouTube (21 million views and counting), among other social networks and websites. The rest, as they say, is history.

Eric Frenchman, John McCain's online consultant and Chief Internet Strategist for the online political agency Connell Donatelli, Inc., commented on the candidates' use of social media throughout the presidential campaign. (His comments were compiled by Jon Clements, who writes the *PR Media Blog*, which can be found at http://pr-media-blog.co.uk.) Keynoting the Future of Digital Marketing event in London in June 2009, Frenchman called search marketing "the great equalizer" and the "one place where you can compete or even beat your competition with less money." He also noted Obama's ability to use Facebook effectively: creating "register to vote" widgets helped him amass over 3 million Facebook followers versus McCain's 610,000. Frenchman also made a point that to us is a key to using social media effectively—rather than use Twitter to engage in conversations with people, McCain used it as a "one-way communication vehicle." In other words, he wasn't listening to his constituents but instead was talking "at" them.

Whether you agree or disagree with the candidates is now moot. The moral of the Obama campaign is this: Inbound marketing, if done right, is a very effective way to reach your prospective customers. How to do inbound marketing right is what you'll learn in this book.

To Do

1. Keep reading this book for "how to" advice.
2. Visit www.barackobama.com and look around.
3. Get fired up to take your market by storm.
4. _____
5. _____
6. _____

(We left these blank for you to write in other "to do's" that come to mind.)

Chapter **2**

Is Your Website a Marketing Hub?

The history of the company website began with the paper brochure that was handed out at trade shows and stuffed into envelopes for mailing to unsuspecting victims (prospects). When the Internet came into play, this same brochure was handed to a web designer who turned it into a beautiful website. This made sense at the time: Brochures were static, the web was new and mostly static, and companies had spent lots of money to have these brochures designed. However, having a "brochureware" website is where the trouble starts for many businesses today.

Megaphone versus Hub

If your website is like many of the websites we see, it is a one-to-many broadcast tool—think *megaphone*. We find that people visit these types of sites once, click around, and never return. Why? Because nothing on these sites, which are filled with sales-oriented messages, compels them to stay.

The web was originally built to be a collaboration platform by Tim Berners-Lee in the 1980s, and while it took a couple of decades to get there, the web is now truly collaborative. Instead of broadcasting to their users with a megaphone, the top-ranked sites today have created communities where like-minded people can connect with each other. In order to take full advantage of this collaborative power, you must rethink your website. Instead of "megaphone," think "hub."

What we want you to do is to change the mode of your website from a one-way sales message to a collaborative, living, breathing hub for your marketplace.

9

It's Not What You Say—It's What Others Say About You

If your company is like most others, you put all your web energy *on* your site. Seventy-five percent of your focus should be on what is happening *off* your website concerning your brand, your industry, and your competitors. Your focus should include creating communities outside of your site for people to connect with you, your products, and others within the community. Ultimately, this "outside" focus will drive people back to your site. The model in Figure 2.1 is of the web—each dot is a website. You want your website to be a large dot that's connected to many other websites—in other words, a hub.

In effect, you want your website to be more like New York City than Wellesley, Massachusetts. NYC has several major highways running through it, three major airports, a huge bus depot, two major train stations, and so on. Wellesley has one highway passing through it, no airport, no bus depot, and no train station. The highways, trains, buses, and airplanes to your site are the search engines, links from other sites, and thousands of mentions of your company in the social media. All of this is what turns your website into a magnetic hub for your industry that pulls people in.

Does Your Website Have a Pulse?

Over time, many people will become regular readers of your website and subscribe to it. These readers won't visit your site directly to read

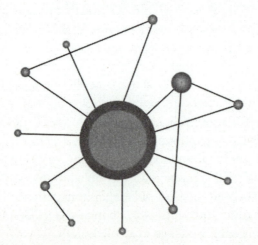

FIGURE 2.1   Internet Model

the content, but will consume your content through a feed reader or RSS reader. RSS (which stands for "really simple syndication") is a technology that allows content to be published and pushed to those users who are subscribed to a feed. RSS makes it very convenient for your readers to automatically know when you have created new content on your site without having to constantly revisit to see if there have been updates.

RSS-enabling your site changes the dynamic of your site from a static brochureware site that someone visits once to a site that's living and breathing. Every time you post something new, your RSS subscribers get that update automatically and are pulled back onto your site.

The same goes for e-mail. Not everyone is up to speed yet on RSS, so you should give site visitors the ability to subscribe to your site or sections of your site via e-mail. In the same way as RSS, this keeps your prospective and current customers in touch with your website—and by extension, you and your company—a totally different paradigm from an online brochure.

As we discuss in later chapters, you want to distribute your site's content to social media sites, such as Twitter and Facebook, where it can spread to new, interested audiences more virally. If you do this properly, people will consume your web content while using these applications, not just on your website.

Your Mother's Impressed, But . . .

If your company is like most others, you are currently in the process of or thinking about redesigning your website. Here is the typical process we see. For the first month or two after the redesign is complete, you *love* your new site and can't stop looking at it. It looks fantastic and your mother is very pleased! Around three months or so later, you start to nitpick about certain things—the navigation is not quite as cool as XYZ Company's, for example. By about six months after the new design, those nitpicks are now starting to really bug you—the background image looks a little dated, and the font choice isn't feeling right anymore. By the time nine months has passed, you start thinking that if you have to look at your site for one more second, you will throw up because you are so sick of that new design. The problem is, you spent a lot of money and the design process took six months, so you don't want to go through all of *that* again—budgets, delays, consensus building, and other matters to address. Then about a year after the new design, something really great happens: You get a new Marketing VP who has the brilliant idea to rebrand the company with new colors, a new logo, tweaked value proposition (verticals this time), and while we are at it, let's get rid of that tired website. Great news—you can start over! Rinse—repeat.

The reality is that most websites *look* perfectly fine. The colors are fine, the menus are fine, the logo is fine, the pictures are fine, and so on. You personally do not like the look of your website because you look at it so often. Your visitors, on the other hand, are not particularly interested in your site's colors or the type of menus used. Your visitors are looking for information—something interesting they can read and learn about—which is why it makes sense to focus on getting people to consume web content through other means such as e-mail, RSS, and social media sites.

Save the thousands of dollars and countless hours you were going to spend on the re*design* of your site and do three things. First, add some collaborative functionality to your site, like a blog (which is easy to update on a regular basis). Second, start creating lots of compelling

TABLE **2.1**   Rethinking Your Website

	Your Website	Inbound Marketing Hub
Interaction	One to many	Many to many
Content	On your domain only	Syndicated across web
Focus	Your website	The rest of the Internet
Consume	Through browser	Browser, mobile
Links	Hundreds	Tens of thousands
Facebook Page	n/a	Thousands of fans
Twitter Account	n/a	Thousands of followers
LinkedIn Group	n/a	Thousands of connections

content people will want to consume (see following chapters on how to do this). Third, start focusing on where the real action is: Google, industry blogs, and social media sites.

Table 2.1 is a summary of the way we want you to start rethinking the current concept of your website.

Tracking Your Progress

Before you begin making the changes we outline in the remainder of this book, take some time to measure where you currently stand in order to track your progress and results as you implement changes.

The first thing you should measure is the number of subscribers you have. By subscribers, we mean people who subscribe to your RSS feed and e-mail list. Also include the number of people who are following you on social media sites, including fans of your Facebook page, members of your LinkedIn Group, and followers on Twitter. If you do not have any subscribers, fans, or followers, don't worry—we discuss how to get them in a later chapter. The more people following/subscribing to you, the broader your reach across your marketplace. This is exceptionally important, particularly in the case where you have some new product innovations that you want to tell your marketplace about or get feedback on.

In addition, you should be measuring the number of links back to your website from other websites and the number of organic keywords that are producing traffic to your site on Google. You can get this information from web analytics software and online tools that measure inbound links, such as grader.com.

The combination of your reach through blog subscribers, social media followers, links into your site, and traffic-producing keywords is the size of your city. You want to make it as easy as possible for people who may be your prospective customers to find your company online. In other words, you want to move from the Wellesley, Massachusetts, model to the New York City model.

Inbound in Action: 37Signals

Based in Chicago, 37Signals builds project management tools, such as the popular Basecamp product, that companies can use to better manage projects. In their early days, the company started the *Signal vs. Noise* blog—and because they wrote compelling content about their industry, readers spread their articles via e-mail and virally through social media, and they were often linked to by other bloggers. Due to this viral activity, 37Signal's blog articles appeared often in Google's search results. Ultimately, the company's blog became among the top 0.1 percent of blogs on the web and helped the company pull in over 3 million users.

If you visit 37Signals today, their website looks nothing like a traditional online brochureware site. Instead, it's an online hub for their industry and includes the company's original industry blog (*Signal vs. Noise*), a product blog, a job board, and information about their products and services. One interesting thing about this site is that the look and feel, colors, menus, and other features haven't changed much since we first noticed them five years ago.

Like 37Signals, you must begin thinking about your web presence in terms of an interactive, constantly changing hub for your entire industry—a hub that also happens to sell a project management product. 37Signals is successful because they leverage the disruptive power of the web to tip the balance of power in their industry from much larger players, such as Microsoft.

While looking at the 37Signals site for inspiration, ask yourself what you can learn. For example, what other types of information, other than product specs, would be useful to your marketplace? What types of information and tools can you put on your site that will pull in more people from your market?

To Do

1. Calculate your reach.
2. Go to grader.com (free) to find out the number of links to your site.
3. Stop obsessing over the way your site looks and feels.
4. Don't spend a bunch of money on a redesign. Start by adding a blog e-mail subscription and comments. Consider making your blog your home page the way Barack Obama does.
5. Check out www.37signals.com.
6. Keep reading to learn how to turn your site from Wellesley to New York City.
7. _____
8. _____
9. _____

Chapter 3

Are You Worthy?

In order to move from outbound to inbound marketing, you need to stop interrupting people in your target market and "get found" by them instead. To do this, you'll need to ensure your company's value proposition is truly *remark*able. What do we mean by "*remark*able"? We borrowed the term from Seth Godin who uses it in place of the word "unique," and we took the liberty of italicizing "*remark*" in order to prompt you to ask yourself whether your product or service is worthy of other people's "*remark*s." Having a remarkable strategy in the inbound marketing era is more critical than ever for two reasons.

First, the Internet enables you to reach many more people than you could pre-Internet, but it also opens you up to potential competitors everywhere (e.g., globally versus locally). The trick is to stand out by becoming as *remark*able (unique and valuable) as possible to a segment of buyers.

Second, the Internet enables *remark*able ideas to spread extremely quickly—far more quickly than pre-Internet days. *Unremark*able ideas languish unfound.

Creating a Remarkable Strategy

We had a brilliant strategy professor at MIT named Arnoldo Hax, who used to frequently repeat the following phrase, "Watch your competitors, but don't follow them." Within your marketplace, unwritten rules form that you and all your competitors implicitly agree to and follow. These rules are typically set by the current market leader who educates the customers—who then forces the rules upon new entrants like you. There are two ways to create a winning strategy in an era where remarkable ideas spread virally and you face more competitors than ever.

The first method is to think across the traditional boundaries of your marketplace to alternatives, not just competitors. A classic example of this type of strategy is the iPod, which is an MP3 player. Before the introduction of the iPod, MP3 players had been around for a long time, but techies, who were the early adopters, were the only people who could figure out how to set them up to play music. The rules in the techie marketplace revolved around feature richness. Apple, on the other hand, didn't follow these "unwritten" rules imposed on the marketplace. Rather than compete with the other MP3 players by making yet another gadget with better/more features, Apple made their MP3 player *much* simpler (and less attractive to the techie MP3 player crowd), integrated it with iTunes, and simplified the down-loading of music. By ignoring the existing unwritten rules and viewing their market across market boundaries, Apple captured a previously untapped market of non-consuming MP3 player users—users who might have stuck with their easy-to-use Sony Walkman rather than "upgrading" to a technically challenging MP3 player.

The second method for creating a winning strategy in the era of inbound marketing is to be the world's best at what you do within your existing market rules. If you are not the world's best within your market, redefine your market more narrowly before one of your competitors takes that position. Take the case of the only monkey wrench manu-facturer in San Diego, who has been selling to plumbers in Southern California his whole life. (We like to use "monkey wrench" as an example—it's not a real business.) The good news about the web is that it enables this manufacturer to get found by plumbers in San Antonio, Texas; San Francisco, California; San Juan, Puerto Rico; San Remo, Italy; and so on. The bad news is that it opens the company up to competitors in all these other cities *and* in Southern California. Rather than compete on the same playing field with hundreds of other monkey wrench manufacturers until the profit margins erode to zero, the owner of the company decides to specialize in monkey wrenches for left-handed plumbers—and eventually becomes the world's best at it. Because far more left-handed plumbers exist around the world than in Southern California, the manufacturer's business explodes. If you cannot rethink your boundaries to get yourself a broad untapped market the way Apple did with the iPod, then you should narrow your boundaries within your existing market and become the world's best within those boundaries.

If you need further help redefining your value proposition, we recommend you read the first few chapters of *Blue Ocean Strategy* by W. Chan Kim and Renée Mauborgne. The ideas presented in that book are quite similar to those of Professor Hax from MIT.

Tracking Your Progress

Progress is particularly hard to measure here! If you have a wide profit margin, then you probably have a *remark*able product offering that matters to a relevant marketplace. If not, keep reading and consult with your advisors until you come up with something truly *remark*able.

Inbound in Action: The Grateful Dead

The Grateful Dead had a *remark*able product. They fused rock and roll with bluegrass and mixed in jazz-style improvisation to create a psychedelic sound. Not only did they have a remarkable sound, they had a remarkable strategy that nicely illustrates both methods described in this chapter.

Rather than compete for mass audiences with the Rolling Stones, Beatles, and other popular bands of its time, the Dead had a remarkable sound that resonated very deeply with a niche audience. They went narrower and deeper with their target market, rather than going broad and shallow against the myriad of other bands.

Most rock and roll bands treated concert tours as a necessary evil required to drive sales of their latest album. The Grateful Dead flipped this assumption on its head and made the concert tours the main revenue driver, and album revenues as upside to it (in fact, they let their concertgoers tape their concerts and pass copies to friends for free). Because they flipped this assumption and focused on the concerts, they had superior sound and light equipment, as well as other concert enhancements, and created a unique experience for their audience that went beyond the typical expectation of what a concert would be like. Most rock band fans buy albums and attend a local concert. The Dead's fans criss-crossed the country, following the band year-round. The Dead crossed boundaries from a rock band to a way of life.

From an early inbound marketing perspective, the Grateful Dead did everything right: They had a remarkable product (sound); they marketed that product to a rabid, niche market; and they ignored conventional wisdom about how to compete for dollars in the music business by making the concert, not album sales, their main revenue source. They ended up creating a movement that transcended the music itself—a strategy that enabled them to be one of the highest-grossing bands of all time.

The strategies employed by the Grateful Dead are more relevant today than ever because the Internet enables information to spread much more easily, which in turn makes traditional markets much more competitive.

Regardless of your musical tastes, you should apply the marketing principles The Grateful Dead used to the products and services you are trying to sell. Begin by asking questions. What are the sacred-cow rules in your industry that should be rethought? Rather than just focusing on competitors, what alternatives can you compete with that cross market boundaries? Rather than trying to expand your market, are you better off shrinking it and increasing profits from a more enthusiastic set of customers?

To Do

1. Go to iTunes and purchase a couple of Grateful Dead songs, including "Space," and note how *remark*able their sound is.
2. Answer the question: "What are you the world's best at?" If the answer is "nothing," rethink your strategy to get narrower or innovate across alternatives.
3. _____
4. _____
5. _____

Part II

Get Found by Prospects

Either write something worth reading about or do something worth writing about.

—*Ben Franklin*

Chapter 4

Create Remarkable Content

Beyond a *remark*able value proposition, you must also create *remark*able content about your company and products, for two important reasons.

First, *remark*able content attracts links from other websites pointing to your website. In other words, you want your content to prompt other content producers on the web to "*remark*" about your products and services and link back to your site. Every one of these links (remarks) gives you a double win: The links send you qualified visitors, and they signal to Google that your website is worthy of ranking for important keywords in your market. More links equals more traffic from relevant sites, in addition to more *free* traffic from Google via search—double win!

Second, remarkable content is easily and quickly spread on social media sites, such as Twitter, Facebook, and LinkedIn. If you create a *remark*able blog article or white paper, it can spread like wildfire within your market.

Building a Content Machine

To make this double win work for your company, you need to create lots of useful, *remark*able content. The people who win really big on the web are the media/content companies (e.g., Wikipedia, *New York Times*, *TechCrunch*) who have a factory for creating new content. Each piece of content that has links to it can be found through those sites linking to it and through Google, and it can be spread virally through social media sites. A savvy inbound marketer learns from the media companies and is half traditional marketer and half content publisher.

The nice thing about *remark*able content with lots of links to it is that the links never go away; as you create more content, it just produces more qualified traffic on top of the traffic you are getting on your older content. *Remark*able content works in the exact opposite way of paid advertising, where you pay and have to keep paying to get more visitors to your site. *Remark*able content is the gift that keeps on giving, so you need to become really good at creating lots of it!

Variety Is the Spice of Life

When you're first getting started, try out different types of content to see what type is the most effective. Different types of content work for different markets. Here are some examples of content to try:

- Blog articles—One-page articles on topics related to your industry.
- White papers—Papers that educate your marketplace on an industry trend, challenge, etc. White papers shouldn't be about products.
- Videos—Short two- to three-minute videos about your industry. Product videos are good too, but do not spread as easily.
- Webinars—Live online presentations on an industry topic, often hosted through online software like WebEx or GoToMeeting.
- Podcasts—Ten- to 20-minute audio programs or interviews with industry experts similar to radio shows.
- Webcasts—Live video shows viewed online.
- Visuals—Content such as infographics and slide decks.

You Gotta Give to Get

The counterintuitive thing about *remark*able content is that the more you give, the more you get. The more *remark*able the content and the more transparent you are about it, the more links to your site and the better it will rank in the search engines. Think about the Grateful Dead from the previous chapter—they gave away lots of content and business came back to them in spades.

You want to move away from the mindset of hiding all of your *remark*able content in your founder's/salesperson's/consultant's head and use that content to attract links to your site, build your brand and attract more people to your business.

Moving Beyond the Width of Your Wallet

Twenty years ago, your marketing effectiveness was a function of the width of your wallet. Today, your marketing effectiveness is a function of the width of your brain. You no longer need to spend tons of money interrupting your potential customers. Instead, you need to *create remark*able content, *optimize* that content (for search engines and social media sites), *publish* the content, *market* the content through blogs and social media, and *measure* what is working and what is not working.

You want to think of yourself as half marketer and half publisher. You might consider making your next full-time marketing hire a writer/journalist, rather than a career marketer.

Tracking Your Progress

You need only track a few simple things to see how well you are doing at creating lots of *remark*able content.

First, track the number of other websites linking to your website. Every time a new website links to yours, it is a vote for your site being *remark*able. Each of these links is like a new road being built to your city and enables more people to find your products and services more easily. You will want to track the number of websites linking to you today and then track this metric over time, as it will give you a sense for whether the marketplace thinks you have increasingly *remark*able things to say!

Second, track the number of times someone shares your content on social media (like Twitter and Facebook). By tracking the number of people who are sharing your site over time, you can get a sense for how *remark*able your content is. If no one is sharing your site, then no one finds the content noteworthy, which means that you probably need to rethink your unique value proposition. If you have a nice increase in the number of people sharing your site or articles, it means that more and more people think your content is interesting and want to return to it.

Third, track the number of pages on your site that have been indexed by Google and are ready to be served on a moment's notice to an eager searcher. The more pages you have in Google's index, the more words you can rank for.

An easy way to track your links, social media presence, and the number of pages indexed by Google is by running your website through the online tool grader.com, which gives all of these numbers for your website in a free report. You ought to check that early and often.

Inbound in Action: Wikipedia

Wikipedia was founded in 2001 on the remarkable premise that the community could collaborate and build a better encyclopedia than an old stalwart like *Encyclopedia Britannica*. How many people told them that it was a stupid idea back in 2001!?

It turns out that there are major benefits to using a collaborative community approach to creating content. Wikipedia can access far more expertise in narrower topics than an organization with a limited set of editors; the site does not kill acres of CO_2-absorbing trees; it has far more articles; and the information is always up to date. In fact, Brian remembers using a 1967 encyclopedia at his house while in grammar school in the late 1970s—it did not have very up-to-date coverage of the Vietnam War for his book report!

Wikipedia has over 32 million pages of content in over 250 languages, and is the fourth most visited site on the Internet, according to Jay Walsh, head of communications for the Wikipedia Foundation. "The information is 100 percent volunteer created," says Jay. Wikipedia is a remarkable project in that we have an enormous amount of information about products, services, events, people—in short, we have everything from mundane information to Shakespeare to World History."

According to Jay, Wikipedia has become an equalizer in that ideas and content can be made better through an editorial process. "Within Wikipedia, anyone and everyone has a chance to design words to describe a thing."

Because Wikipedia has become indispensable, it has over six million links from other websites *remark*ing about it. That is six million different pages on the web, which people can click on and find themselves on Wikipedia's site. Because of the sheer volume of links into Wikipedia and the fact that it's a *remark*able content factory, Google considers it an authoritative site.

What can you learn from Wikipedia? Can you get your users, customers, partners, and suppliers to create *remark*able content for you? Could you set up an industry-specific wiki off of your website, moderated by your business and contributed to by your entire industry?

To Do

1. Think of your marketing function as half marketer and half publisher.
2. Start creating *remark*able content on an ongoing basis.
3. Go to grader.com and note the number of linking sites, social shares of your site, and number of pages Google has indexed.
4. _____
5. _____
6. _____

Chapter **5**

Get Found in the Blogosphere

As we discussed earlier, to be an effective inbound marketer, it's important you create lots of *remark*able content. A great way to do that is by starting a blog.

Blogging makes sense for many types of businesses for many reasons. First, a blog will help establish your company as a thought leader in your market. Second, due to its dynamic nature and the fact you're creating new content on a regular basis, a blog will change your website from an online brochure to a living, breathing hub for your marketplace. Third, a blog gives your potential customers a way to engage with you versus being hit with a premature sales pitch; by conversing with your potential customers via your blog, you build trust over time, so that when you actually talk to them about your product and service offerings, they're prepared to hear from you. Fourth, a blog will dramatically improve your search engine rankings; a blog is a great way to create more pages on your site (each article is a page), and the more pages Google has, the more your site shows up in the search engine results pages (SERPs) for dozens of keywords. And, because search engines like to see sites linking to one another, a blog helps your search engine results because other bloggers are far more likely to link to a *remark*able blog article about your industry than to the products page on your website. The more inbound links pointing to your site, the more traffic comes your way and the more Google views your site as an "authorative hub"—and thus the higher your site goes in the SERPs.

Getting Your Blog Started Right

Many blogging platforms and tools exist to help you quickly set up a blog. The most popular of these is WordPress.com.

Whichever platform you choose, however, it's imperative that your blog is hosted on your *own* domain, not that of the platform provider (whereby your website address is something like mygreatsite .wordpress.com). It's fine to use WordPress, but the problem with hosting off of their domain is that you're building search authority for the WordPress.com domain—not for your company. We recommend having your blog address (or URL) be yourcompany.com/blog or blog.yourcompany.com (techies call this a subdomain). Most of the free blogging tools allow you to set up your own domain (usually for a very small annual fee).

Another option is to name your blog based on your topic rather than your business. You would then register a new domain for your blog and put your blog there. However, giving your blog its own separate domain can be a bit tough if your financial and/or staff resources are tight, as managing this second—and separate—brand can be a fair amount of work. You'd also then be working on building SEO authority (which we talk about in Chapter 6) for *two* domains.

One thing you'll want to do with your blog is ensure people can leave comments and subscribe to your blog via RSS and e-mail. (Yes, many people do want to be alerted to new blog posts via e-mail.)

Authoring Effective Articles

Now that you have set your blog up, let's get cranking.

To have a successful blog that people will look forward to reading, we recommend that you focus your blog posts on your industry. If you're in the security software business, for example, we recommend you write about security software and not fall into the temptation of including articles about your weekend ski trip, your Red Sox Nation membership, your kids' pictures, or your coin collection. The length of your articles can vary widely—we've seen both short and long articles succeed. The key is to make the articles useful.

What should you write about? Anything that pertains to your industry and that will be of interest to your readers: how-to articles, analysis of a current industry trend or challenge, announcements of upcoming events, feedback on articles you read in print publications, and so on.

In addition to informative articles, you can include lots of other information that mixes things up nicely for your readers. Give your readers a list of links to 5 or 10 other relevant articles you've recently read or videos you've watched. Build on another blogger's work by adding to the discussion with your own insight or disagree with another blogger—this is a great way to get attention from the top bloggers in your industry. Diversify your blog posts by adding video—either embed links to existing YouTube videos or break out the video camera and record yourself talking about a hot industry topic, but keep it short—no more than two to three minutes, max! Create cartoons or caricatures of things happening in your industry. For inspiration, take a look at the funny cartoons in the Sunday *New York Times* that parody politicians, and then find an artist who can create something similar for your industry. Buy a copy of the *New Yorker* magazine, take a look at the cartoons, and try to find someone to create similarly humorous ones about your own industry.

In order to come up with consistently good ideas for your blog, you'll have to figure out the way in which you work best. For example, Brian tends to get his best ideas on Saturday morning after a good night's sleep, but Dharmesh finds good ideas all the time. In order to keep track of your ideas, either carry a notebook and pen with you or use your mobile device to store ideas. Brian, for example, likes to write himself an e-mail on his iPhone to jot down new blog ideas. The best way to find ideas, however, is to learn from other bloggers by reading their blogs.

In addition to your own blog content, you'll want to invite others to write on your blog, including local professors interested in your industry, thoughtful customers, analysts in your industry, and other bloggers in your industry. Guest blog articles make sense for a few reasons: They expose your company to thought-leaders in your industry who will be flattered by your invitation, providing you a chance to engage them in a deeper way than if you just cold called them; guest articles lessen your content creation load; and they expose your audience to more ideas that (hopefully) reinforce your *remark*able value proposition. The upside for guest bloggers is that they get exposed to a new audience and get a link from your blog back to theirs. In some cases, if the guest blogger is *really* well known it may even make sense to pay them for their efforts.

When you ask someone to be a guest author, you might get some "pushback," as people are busy and don't always have the time to write a new article (especially if they are prolific bloggers themselves!). To help people develop content for your blog, you can use the following tactics: Send interview questions via e-mail to which they respond, and you paste into an article; or purchase an inexpensive video camera (such as the Flip Camera) and record yourself interviewing your guest—it can be rather fun pretending to be Charlie Rose or Anderson Cooper for an hour.

New bloggers often feel anxiety about how frequently they need to write. As a rule of thumb, we recommend you write a minimum of once per week. If you're a sole business owner, you'll have to take this on yourself. If you work for a larger company or partnership, we recommend you spread the work around. For example, in a security software company, the CEO, CTO, product manager, and application engineer can rotate weekly—with each person writing one article a month. The benefit of spreading the work around is that it takes the workload off you, and it gives exposure to rising stars in your organization who will probably enjoy the privilege.

Above all else, make sure your articles are *remark*able!

Help Google Help You

We discuss search engine optimization (SEO) in Chapter 6, but it's worth touching on it now in the context of how you write your blog articles.

With regard to SEO, the most important part of your article is the title. Each individual article is its own page that sits in Google's index to be retrieved for an eager searcher. When Google matches what is being searched with all the pages in its index, one of the most important things it tries to do is match the article title with the phrase being searched. If you want your article to rank number one for the term "left-handed monkey wrench" in Google, then your article title ought to contain that phrase. Having a keyword phrase in the article title is not a guarantee that your article will rank well for that phrase, but it's very helpful.

Within the text of your article, look for important keyword phrases that describe your industry and turn them into hyperlinks. Techies call the words you can click on "anchor text." For example, if in the text of your article you have the phrase "world's best security software," then you ought to make that phrase a link that points to your home page or to another good article on your blog on that topic. The words Google and other search engines see in those hyperlinks help them understand the relevance of the page you are linking to.

If you are already a blogger, we recommend you start a project where you go back to all of your old blog articles and rework the titles to include relevant industry keywords, as well as find opportunities to create links from old articles to your website or other articles.

Making Your Articles Infectious

If you want your articles to be read and spread, then you need to get really good at crafting catchy article titles. Many copywriting experts recommend that you spend half your time writing the article and half your time writing a catchy title.

Why is the title so important? Well, most people will find your article through their e-mail inbox, in search, or on social media. We live in a society where every person has massive information overload, so your article needs to capture their attention in literally half a second. Think about how and why you click on certain articles—it's usually because the headline captured your attention. When you look at a Google screen with 10 results, for example, do you click on all 10 or just the first one that catches your eye? While on Facebook, do you click on someone's link every time or do you glance at the title first and only click on it if it really catches your attention? (See Figure 5.1.)

Remember, your articles are competing with hundreds of other pieces of information, so the title needs to be irresistible. Here are the titles of a few blog articles of ours that have gone viral:

8 Marketing Tips from an Olympic Gold Medalist

10 Leadership Lessons from Don Corleone

Steve Jobs and Guy Kawasaki—PowerPoint Best Practices

7 Signs You Should Run Screaming from an SEO Consultant

Innovation	
Show: 25 new items - all items	Mark all as read	Refresh	Folder settings... ▾
☆ Product Marketing Blog	**Living in an Agile World** - We've been working with our friends at Enthios
☆ Don Dodge on The Next Bi	**The best 7 minutes of your day** - After years in this business we can bec
☆ Presentation Zen	**"Good" visual examples to get you thinking** - Recently I stumbled acros
☆ How to Change the World	**Pictures from My Reign in Spain** - Just returned from my first visit to Barc
☆ Product Marketing Blog	**Friday fun: Facebook now the 5th largest country** - Facebook posted so
☆ Presentation Zen	**Mix 09: Bill Buxton on Design & Return on Experience** - You may not ha
☆ Product Marketing Blog	**Doing the impossible** - Every time I tried to initiate change in my company
☆ blog.payne.org	**Proprietary Distribution Doesn't Win** - The blogosphere is aflutter with th
☆ Don Dodge on The Next Bi	**Freemium model for newspapers and other survival ideas** - Newspape
☆ Don Dodge on The Next Bi	**Ashton Kutcher first with 1 Million followers on Twitter** - Twitter traffic i
☆ OnStartups	**Startup Marketing: Tactical Tips From The Trenches** - I'm speaking at th
☆ HighContrast	**Fastignite is born** - Spring time. Time for changes. I've moved on from Po
☆ blog.payne.org	**Senior Folks Looking for Startup Jobs** - With the recession, inbound req

FIGURE **5.1**   Inbox Overload

How to Convince a CEO to Enter Twenty-First Century Internet Marketing

12 Quick Tips to Search Google Like an Expert

These articles went viral because several of them are numbered lists—for some reason our species is drawn to numbered lists (e.g., Top 7 Reasons [blank] Is Going to Be Dead in 10 Years), so you might as well use this to your advantage. The articles also went viral because the titles mention famous companies (e.g., Google) or famous people (e.g., Don Corleone)—these tend to do better than ones that do not. Think about magazines at the grocery checkout: The headlines grab our attention because they shout out over-the-top "news."

Give Your Articles a Push

Now that you've spent time writing a good article with a great title, you'll want to market it so the most people possible will read it. Twitter, Facebook, and LinkedIn all have a small form that lets you post a "status update" that is shared with your friends and followers. You can post the link to your article on each of these social networks, and encourage your readers to share it. We also recommend that you encourage your users who are on myriad social bookmarking sites (Reddit, Stumble-Upon, etc.) to post and vote on your article by having these relevant icons on your site as well. If your blog is about left-handed monkey wrenches, it might not make sense to have an icon pointing to Digg or Reddit, but it does make sense to have icons for Twitter, Facebook, LinkedIn, and StumbleUpon.

Many industries have their own social bookmarking sites and/or discussion forums (like LinkedIn Groups). For your industry, you want to find these forums and make sure you post your good articles there for others to comment on as well.

If you're just getting started with your blog and do not have any followers, then we recommend that you *e-mail* a link to your article to a subset of your personal e-mail contacts who you think might be interested. Your e-mail should contain a link to the article and a request asking your contacts to forward it, comment on it, post it on their favorite social site, and subscribe to the blog if they enjoyed it. This gets very old very fast, so use this tactic only with exceptional articles and only when you are first getting started.

Starting Conversations with Comments

You should encourage readers to leave comments, especially if they disagree with you. When readers come to your blog article and see a lot of comments, they assume the content is good and are more likely to read the article and enter the conversation through the comments section of the article. If you don't ask your readers to comment, they're less likely to do so. The call-to-action at the bottom of every blog post should state something like, "Please let me know your thoughts in the comments section below."

When first starting a blog, it can be disconcerting to think that others can openly comment on your thoughts, products, market, and so on. However, it's actually quite rare for an unhappy customer or a competitor to rant in your blog comments. If they do, we recommend you let those comments stay, as they give you a public opportunity to handle objections and exhibit your customer service skills. If you do not feel comfortable with that idea, almost all blogging systems these days give you the ability to delete a comment once it's been posted.

Avoid the temptation to turn on your blog's comment moderation feature (comment moderation lets you approve comments before they appear on your blog), as this extra step in the process creates just enough friction to ensure that meaningful conversations cannot really take place. Comment moderation also discourages your active readers from commenting on later articles. Similarly, we recommend that you do not turn off comments altogether.

Most blogging systems will send you an e-mail when someone leaves a comment, so that you can respond quickly. If someone has taken the time to leave you a comment (which often takes the form of a question), do respond to the comment in order to get a discussion going on your site. These discussions will attract a lot more qualified prospects than the product page on your website!

Why Blogs Sometimes Fail

The most frequent reason blogs fail is because the author or company writing the blog oversells their product or service. You want your blog to turn your website into a hub for your industry, not just be an advertisement for your product. The idea is to pull your industry in with useful, brilliant content in the hope that prospects connect the dots down the road, see that you are the most thoughtful person in your industry on the topic, and eventually buy from you.

The Gift That Keeps on Giving

Blogs are almost never an overnight success—they build cumulatively over time. Every time you write an article that has links into it from other sites, that article can get found by people browsing the web on those other sites forever. That same article can get found by searchers in Google for various search terms forever. That article might also attract visitors who might subscribe to your blog. The great thing about that blog article is that the page, the Google rankings, the links, and the subscriber are all durable assets. Once you write that article, it gives you value forever. When you write your second article, the same thing happens. And so on. A blog is a durable asset that delivers durable value that lasts.

If you spend your energy and money on advertising this month, you will get some traffic from it, but you will have to pay again next month to get more. The blog article delivers value on a semi-permanent basis.

Because the benefits accrue over time and are nonlinear, it is easy to give up after a few posts. Our advice would be to stick with it.

Consuming Content with RSS

Now that we have covered how to create content on your own blog, let's shift our attention to how to engage potential customers on other blogs in your industry. This can work whether you have a blog or not!

Your first step is to find a good RSS reader, an essential tool for the inbound marketer, as it gives you the ability to keep track of many relevant blogs without having to revisit them constantly to see if new articles have been posted. It is relatively important that you keep on top of new content that comes out, as we describe in the comments section further on.

You can choose from many RSS readers, but we recommend Feedly. It's free, and completely web-based, so there's nothing to download. To sign up, go to http://feedly.com. When a new article becomes available for a blog that you subscribe to, that blog will be highlighted in bold in your reader. An RSS reader works like a parallel e-mail inbox in that it fills with articles of interest from your favorite sites as soon as they become available.

Subscribe to Relevant Industry Blogs

Go to Google's blog search engine and type in the phrase or acronym that best describes your industry. Start clicking on the ones that sound interesting and subscribe to them with your RSS reader.

If only a few blogs exist for your industry, subscribe to all of them. If you find thousands, then use grader.com to determine which blogs have mojo and which do not. A high Website Grade (e.g., > 90) means the blogger has lots of followers and high authority, so engaging on this blog will get you more leverage than engaging with a lesser-known blogger. Think about this process as though you were a lion hunting for elephants (customers). You want to hang around the watering hole (blog) where the most elephants come to drink and bathe.

Contribute to the Conversation

Now that you have subscribed to the relevant, authoritative blogs in your industry, make reading them a standard part of your daily regimen. Every morning when you get your cup of coffee, open your RSS reader for 20 minutes while you boost your energy level! Reading articles through an RSS reader is much like reading a newspaper, but much more efficient. Quickly scan the titles looking for interesting stuff and dive down where your attention is drawn. A good way to get in the habit of doing this is to stop your subscription to your daily print newspaper and start taking your morning dose of news through RSS.

When you see an article relevant to your business, leave a thoughtful comment—one that extends the thoughts of the author in a meaningful way, perhaps by way of a perfect example. A thoughtful comment can also disagree with the author's article, so long as it is credible. Bloggers tend to like disagreement in the comments as it draws in more people. A thoughtful comment is not a two-word comment such as "great article," nor is it a blatant advertisement about your company's product such as "Come visit www.yourcompany.com." When you leave a comment, we recommend that you fill in the standard fields for name, e-mail, website, and comment. Once your comment is posted, your website address will automatically show up, so there is no need to re-type it in the comment itself.

Why do you want to do all of this commenting? Two reasons. First, you want the author of the blog to notice and appreciate your comment and then wander over to your website (or blog) for a look. If the author does this more than once and finds your value proposition remarkable, he or she will often end up writing about your offerings and linking to your site. This link gives your site more authority in the eyes of Google— which in turn moves your site up in the rankings for relevant keywords.

Second, commenting on blogs gives you relevant traffic. If readers of a blog appreciate your comment, they will often click through to your blog or website—thus sending you prospects. Remember, the more relevant and higher authority of the blog (based on grader.com), the more readers it will have who will hopefully click over and read your site.

The reason we're advocating that you read blog content through an RSS reader is based on timeliness. If the blog you're commenting on is very popular, it will have many comments posted to it literally minutes after the post goes live. If you're the 15th comment, your likelihood of

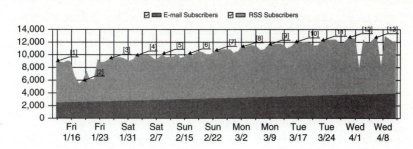

FIGURE 5.2 Subscriber Totals

being found by readers who are scanning down at the comments goes way down. You want to be one of the first people to comment.

Tracking Your Progress

You can track several metrics to determine the success of your blog. First, measure the number of subscribers over time (blog + e-mail) (see Figure 5.2).

Next, track the number of visitors to your blog (blog.yourcompany.com) over time, the number of qualified leads over time that came from your blog, and the number of new customers you signed up who originally found you via your blog (see Figure 5.3). You should take the visitors/leads/customers via the blog metric and compare that to other new channels such as Google and social media sites (inbound), as well as old (outbound) channels such as advertising, trade shows, cold calls, and others. After 6 to 12 months of following these steps, your blog will end up being one of the best sources of customers you have.

You should also track each individual article along the following dimensions: date, author, visitors, comments, and links. When you have this information together, you can do some interesting analyses. For example, you can sort the articles by each success metric to determine which article titles are getting the most interest, which authors are doing

Referrer	Visitors ▾	Leads	Conv.%	Customers
Google [search]	44,642	2,140	4.79%	64
blog.hubspot.com	39,201	4,646	11.85%	33

FIGURE 5.3 Blog Funnel Analysis

ARTICLE	PUBLISHED	AUTHOR	PAGE GRADE™	COMMENTS ▼	INBOUND LINKS	PAGE VIEWS
Web 2.0: On Bubbles and Business Models	2 years ago	Dharmesh Shah	2	275	8	294
Go West, Young Entrepreneur! Is The Valley Better For Software Statups?	2 years ago	Dharmesh Shah	9	226	11	223
Back to Basics: User Generated Revenue As A Business Model	2 years ago	Dharmesh Shah	2	216	7	234

FIGURE 5.4   Blog Analysis

the best work, and so forth. You can use this information to consistently improve your blog content over time (see Figure 5.4).

A good proxy for how you are doing in the blogosphere is to measure the number of links back to your site over time, and measure the amount of traffic you get from links from blogs (see Figure 5.5).

Inbound in Action: Whole Foods

We can't tell you how many times we've heard that Internet marketing will not work in an "old school" marketplace. It doesn't get much older school than the grocery food business, yet organic seller Whole Foods Market is using its *Whole Story* blog to "share some of the cool things going on inside the company as well as the natural foods industry," according to Paige Brady, the senior coordinator of the Integrated Media Editorial Team for Whole Foods Market. You can find their blog at blog.wholefoodsmarket.com.

Instead of simply posting store hours or coupons on their site the way many grocery stores do, Whole Foods is creating remarkable content on its blog that pulls in new customers, enables them to

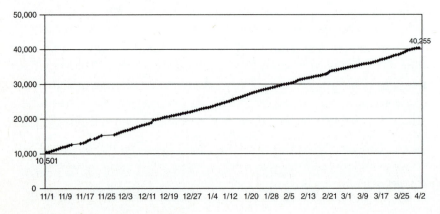

FIGURE 5.5   Tracking Inbound Links

connect more deeply with those customers, and makes it easier for customers to spread the word. Whole Foods is doing many things right on their blog, so let's go through some of their best practices.

Whole Food's content is *remark*able. Because Whole Foods has been creating remarkable content since July 2006, its blog is now a major, sustainable asset to them with over 7,500-plus pages in Google's index eligible to rank for different search terms. Over 12,000 other websites link to these 7,500 pages, giving Whole Foods 12,000 ways in which new customers can find them. This relatively large number of links tells Google that the Whole Foods blog is worthy of ranking for many important terms. Whole Foods also has tens of thousands of blog subscribers who get notified and sent a link every time the company posts a new article. The pages, the links, and subscribers are a major *permanent asset* to Whole Foods.

In our opinion, they set up their domain right: blog.wholefoods market.com. Rather than create a new brand to keep track of, they made the blog a subdomain of their main website—a practice that's very common. According to Brady, the company is lucky to have a "whole bunch of smart, passionate people doing incredible work in all areas like organics, supporting local growers, green practices, Fair Trade, micro-lending, and all kinds of food-related stuff. We have a chief 'hunter-gatherer' for the blog to make sure we don't miss important stores and we invite our team member experts to write their own posts as well." Content on Whole Story includes straight articles, guest recipes, contests, and video and is created by over 20 employees.

Whole Foods is particularly adept at writing clever, short article titles that are easy to spread virally within the social mediasphere, including:

Natural Approaches to Allergies

And the Green Prom Winner Is . . .

Pregnancy—A Time to Go Natural

The combination of pithy titles and good articles is one reason why the company has over 3.6 million Twitter followers and over 1.5 million Facebook fans.

Brady adds that another important aspect of the blog is "continuing the conversation through comments from our readers. We have an educated customer base and they ask excellent questions, which we answer either in the comments section or by posting a new blog entry. It's very important to us that we engage with our readers." The proof is in the pudding, as they say, as *Whole Story* is read by tens of thousands of subscribers.

The *Whole Story* team are masters of the soft sell. It is very hard to acquire subscribers and get lots of other websites to remark about you if your blog is overtly selling your products. Approximately 90 percent of Whole Foods' blog content does not sell their products at all. A great example of a soft sell article is one concerning a sheep's milk cheese called Mons-Cazelle de Saint Affrique. Instead of talking about the product itself (and why people should buy it) the cheese buyer wrote about the romantic town in which the cheese is made, how it's made, and the people who make it. The article ends with the following: "Either way it is a fantastic cheese that we are offering you during the month of April. Welcome spring with a lovely, young cheese from France, and hurry since it may not be around long!" (see Figure 5.6).

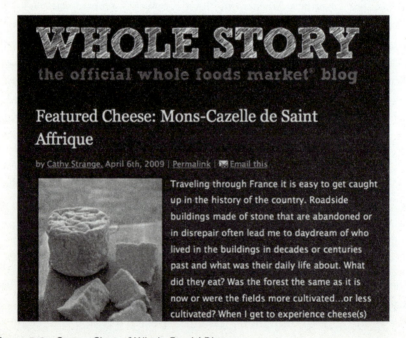

FIGURE 5.6   Screen Shot of Whole Foods' Blog

To Do

1. Set up your blog as blog.yourdomain.com or a "net" new domain (not _.blogger.com or wordpress.com).
2. Start creating remarkable content in different flavors (articles, videos, links, guest blogs) with search-friendly, catchy titles.
3. Market that content through e-mail, RSS, and the social mediasphere.
4. Measure subscribers to the blog, measure blog conversion to leads/customers, and measure individual blog articles for best practices.
5. Be patient.
6. Set up Google Reader.
7. Find and subscribe to industry blogs.
8. Unsubscribe to your daily newspaper.
9. Start commenting thoughtfully on other blogs.
10. When you have your coffee every day, read your RSS feeds.
11. Check out blog.wholefoodsmarket.com as an example of a good blog.
12. _____
13. _____
14. _____

Chapter 6

Get Found in Google

How many times did you use Google to look for something today? Chances are, several times. In fact, every day, there are approximately 5.9 billion Google searches. It's likely that amongst all those billions of searches, some were related to *your* product or service. Simply put, if your site isn't being found on Google, you're missing a major opportunity to generate leads for your business. In fact, you're probably sending these leads to your competitors!

Other than the sheer volume of potential visitors you can draw through Google, there's another important consideration for ensuring your site ranks well: People searching on Google are actually *looking for something*. This may sound a bit obvious, but contrast this to getting traffic from blogs. Blog readers are often focused on learning something or being entertained. They often don't have a specific goal. Google searchers, on the other hand, are looking for something. Sometimes they are searching for a product or service. Sometimes they're searching for information. But, they do have a specific goal. If what they are searching for is related to your business, you want to be found.

Paid versus Free

When users conduct Google searches, two kinds of results appear on the SERP (search engine results page): the "organic" search results (also known as "natural" results) and the paid or sponsored results. Generally, the paid results, or Sponsored Links, appear on the right side of the SERP, and sometimes at the top (see Figure 6.1).

These Sponsored Links are essentially advertising—which is why the Sponsored Links are often referred to as "pay per clicks ads."

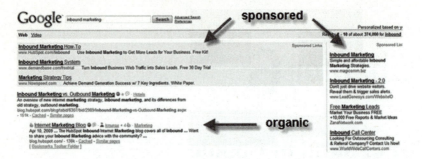

Figure 6.1   Screen Shot of Organic and Sponsored Google Search Results

Organizations can bid for placement in Google search results by purchasing Google AdWords, a pay per click (PPC) advertising program. Here's how it works: You offer to pay Google a certain cost per click (CPC) anytime your ad is shown to searchers based on what keyword they searched on. You pay for how often people click on your ad and visit your website—not how often your ad is shown (impressions). For example, say you were a tax attorney in Boston and wanted to reach Google users that searched on the term "Boston Tax Attorney." You could buy that Google AdWord and offer $2.50 per click. This means that if your ad is shown to users, you pay Google $2.50 every time someone clicks on your ad. The price that you offer (or bid) determines whether your ad will be shown, where it will be shown, and how many times. The price that you need to pay depends on how many other people are also interested in that same keyword. Google AdWords is an auction that's held in real-time. Those companies willing to pay more are more likely to get their ad shown in the limited amount of real estate Google has available for these paid AdWords ads. It's important to note that Google also uses the *quality* of an ad, in addition to the bid price, to determine ad placement. High quality ads that meet the needs of searchers can pay less on a per-click basis.

That's how paid search works. You pay Google to send visitors to your website, and how much you pay is based on how many other people are competing for those same searchers.

On the other hand, the organic or natural results are not based on payment, but on the quality of the content and what Google believes would be the most valuable pages for their users. When your web page shows up in the organic results, and users click on your link and visit your web page, these clicks are essentially free (you don't pay anything to Google when people click on a link to your site). Clearly, all things being equal, you'd rather your business get visitors from Google for free, wouldn't you? It actually gets even better than that. Not only is placement in the organic results free, but visitors click on these results much more often than they do the paid results. Research from MarketingSherpa and Enquiro show that 75 percent of searchers click the organic listings while 25 percent click on the paid results.[1] This means you'll likely get much more traffic if you can rank for certain keywords organically than if you were to try to buy your way into the paid results for those same words.

Clearly, you'd prefer to get free traffic instead of paying for it. That's what search engine optimization (SEO) is all about. You want to increase the chances *your* web pages will show up as high as possible in the Google results when a user searches for a keyword related to your business.

By default, when users type a search term into Google, 10 results or listings are shown per page. This means the first page of results shows the top 10 results, the second page shows the next 10 results, and so on. It's important to note that getting on the first page of Google is very important, because the first page gets a lion's share of the traffic for that keyword. A recent study shows that Google's first page captures over 89 percent of the traffic, and most users will not look beyond the first page. Even within the first page, the traffic is not spread evenly—the top-ranked result (number one on the first page) captures about 42 percent of the traffic. The higher you rank for a given term, the more visitors to your website, and the difference between the number of visitors does not occur in small increments—it's significant. So, you want to do your best to rank as high as possible for the keyword that you care about.

The practice of understanding how search engines work, and striving to get a website to rank well for keywords, is known as search engine optimization (SEO). The rest of this chapter looks at the basics of SEO and how you can leverage this practice to get more visitors to your website.

---

[1] Organic versus paid search; www.hubspot.com/organic-vs-paid-search/; www.enquiroresearch.com/eyetracking-report.aspx.

A (Brief) Introduction to How Google Works

To succeed with search engine optimization, and rank for keywords you care about, it's necessary to understand a little about how Google works.

Google does two basic things. First, it crawls the Internet looking for web pages, storing these pages in its index. Think of the Google index as a massive catalog (much like a library would have a catalog of every book). Second, it has software that processes user searches and finds the best matching web pages from its index.

In order for your web page to rank well in Google for a given keyword, two things need to happen. First, Google needs to crawl and index your web page. If your web page isn't being crawled, you're not even in the race! Then, of all the possible web pages that Google thinks is a match for the keyword being searched, your page or pages have to be considered *better* than the other possible candidates.

Getting Google to visit a web page and index it is not as hard to do as it once was. In the early days of SEO, it was often necessary to manually submit new web pages to Google and the other search engines so they would know these pages existed. Many SEO consultants and software tools offered this as a service called search engine submission. Today, manual submission of pages is rarely necessary. Instead, simply getting a link to a new web page from a page that is already being crawled by Google is sufficient to get the new page crawled as well. That's how most new pages get into the Google index today. If you do decide you want to manually submit your pages to Google, it's free and easy (and should not involve hiring a consultant). Just use the Google Add URL tool (www.Google.com/addurl).

Getting web pages indexed by Google is not the problem. Getting them to *rank well* is where the challenge is. To understand how to rank well, it's helpful to understand the basics of how the Google ranking algorithm works.

How Google's Brain Works

Let's dig into how Google's software brain works. We promise not to make it too technical, and you'll know enough to impress your friends and family at the next holiday party.

When a user types a keyword into Google's search box, Google first looks through the billions of pages in its index and comes up with a list of results that are matches for the term. For example, if you type *inbound marketing* into the Google search box, there are currently about 1,060,000 pages that Google finds related to that term. Once Google has this list of pages, it sorts the list so the highest-quality results are at the top of the list and the lowest-quality results are at the bottom.

Ranking is based on a combination of two things, *relevance* and *authority*. The *relevance* is a measure of how close of a match a given web page is to the term being searched. This is based on factors such as the title tag (sometimes called the "page title"), the page content, and the anchor text of links to the page. The *authority* of a page is a measure of how important and authoritative that given page is in the eyes of Google.

The authority of a web page is at the heart of the Google algorithm. Google calls this authority PageRank™, named for Larry Page, one of the founders of Google. The idea behind PageRank is brilliantly simple and based on work at Stanford University on how to measure the credibility and importance of academic papers. The authority of a given academic paper can be determined by the number of *other* papers that cite and reference it. The more citations a given paper has, the better the paper. However, not all citations are created equal. A citation from another paper that itself has a high number of citations is considered to carry more weight. High-authority papers are cited by other high-authority papers. It is this same principle that drives Google's PageRank, but instead of academic papers, it's about web pages. And instead of citations, it's about links from other web pages. The authority of a web page is calculated based on the number of inbound links from other web pages and the authority of *those* pages.

Here's a simple example. Let's say you've created a web page about the best restaurants in Boston. If your page is just sitting out there, and nobody is linking to it, Google assigns a relatively low authority score to your page. This is not surprising. Google has no evidence that you know what you're talking about or that your content is of high quality. Over time, a few other bloggers find your web page and link to it from their pages. This causes your authority to increase. The more powerful the web pages that link to you, the more your authority goes up. Now, if someday, Boston.com (the website for the *Boston Globe*) links to your page, your authority goes up significantly. Why? Because Boston.com itself is a high-authority website.

So, to get SEO authority, the name of the game is to get as many links as possible from as many high-authority sites as possible. How do you get links? By creating *remark*able content.

YOUR CONTENT IS NOT WORTHY. *NO RANK FOR YOU!*

Search engine optimization when done well is *not* about tricking Google into ranking your web page. It's about creating content that users would *want* to find and helping Google deliver great search results. The best way to rank well in the Google search results is to create content that is rank-worthy. By rank-worthy, we mean content that is *worthy* of being ranked because it is what the user who is searching would consider to be of high quality and relevance.

Picking the Perfect Keywords

The first step in search engine optimization is deciding which keywords to optimize your site for. Keywords are what users type into the search box for their search query. Three primary criteria go into selecting the right keywords to optimize your website: relevance, volume, and difficulty.

RELEVANCE

You want to pick keywords related to your business. When crafting your list of possible keywords, it is best to think from the prospect's perspective. Try to think about what keywords a prospect looking for your product or service is likely to type into Google. Come up with many different variations.

ESTIMATED SEARCH VOLUME

Even if you get the number one spot in the Google search results for a keyword, it doesn't guarantee you're going to get lots of visitors to your website. The amount of traffic you will drive to your website is dependent on how many people search on that keyword. To pick great keywords, you need to have a sense for the approximate number of times users search for that word in Google. Check the resources section at the end of the book for information on tools you can use to help with determining search volume for keywords.

DIFFICULTY

This is a measure of how hard it will be to rank for the keyword, based on the strength of the competition and your own website's authority. Ranking well in Google is a competition. Of the thousands of web pages trying to rank for a given keyword, only 10 can make it to the front page. So, if you have a new website and are trying to break in to the top 10, you'll have to displace someone else. For some keywords, this is relatively easy to do, if the existing top 10 are relatively weak. For competitive keywords, the strength of the competition may be high, and ranking on the first page may be very difficult.

Picking the best keywords is an exercise in balancing these three factors: relevance, search volume, and difficulty. You shouldn't just solve for one factor. For example, picking a relevant keyword that has very high search volume is not going to mean much if the difficulty is so high that you'll never be able to rank. Similarly, picking very easy words that have very weak competition is not going to generate much traffic if only a few people a month use that term to search.

When picking your keywords, you should start with a list of relevant keywords for your business. Then, determine what the esti-mated volume is for those keywords and how much competition there is for that keyword. If you're just getting started, you should probably begin with keywords that have relatively low competition. If your website doesn't have much authority yet in the eyes of Google, you're unlikely to rank well for a highly competitive keyword. In addition, if you don't make it into the first page of the search results, you are not likely to get much traffic from those keywords. Choose keywords that have relatively low competition instead. Then, as you build authority for your web pages, and start ranking for these keywords, you can move up to higher volume keywords that have more competition.

When coming up with your initial list of keyword candidates, it is important to think from the viewpoint of your potential customers. Don't just think about how you would describe your business, think about what users *searching* for your business might type into Google. For example, you might describe yourself as "interior design for businesses." You'd then come up with several variations on interior design, and maybe even interior decoration (because users often confuse the two). However, perhaps some of your potential customers don't use the phrase "interior design." Instead, they might use "office space design." The key is to put yourself in the shoes of your potential customer. A very effective way to know how your customers might search for you is to watch them. If you have an existing website that gets traffic from Google, you can use analytics software to see what terms visitors are already using to get to your site. This doesn't work well if your site is poorly optimized and the only traffic you're getting from Google are people searching on your company name. In most cases, looking at this kind of data yields new insights into potential keywords that you can add to your list.

Using PPC for Better Data

If you have even a modest budget, you should consider launching a small PPC (pay-per-click) advertising campaign to determine what your best keywords might be. This is particularly useful if you are just getting started and don't know which keywords will work. When you run a PPC campaign, you can pick a set of keywords and begin generating traffic almost *immediately*. Often, with SEO, it can take weeks or months before you rank well enough for certain keywords to see any traffic. Further, you can channel the traffic to a specific web page, such as a landing page (discussed later). This way, you can measure what the *conversion rate* is for traffic from various keywords. The benefit of getting this conversion data is that you can make even better decisions as to which keywords to pick. Remember, the purpose of inbound marketing is not just to get more traffic to your website, but to convert more of that traffic into qualified leads and customers.

On-Page SEO: Doing the Easy Stuff First

Once you've picked your list of target keywords, the next step is to start using these keywords on your website.

On-page factors that influence rankings are those contained within the page that you are trying to rank. These are factors that you can control directly by modifying your web pages and as such, are the easiest factors to address to improve your SEO.

THE POWER OF THE PAGE TITLE TAG

Of the elements on the page that influence Google, by far, the most important is the page title. The page title is what shows up at the top of the browser window (and is used for the text of the link in search results). In Figure 6.2, the page title tag is shown above the URL at the top ("Content Distribution Management software—Signiant").

Given the importance of the Page Title tag to SEO, it's worth spending a fair amount of time crafting great titles for your most important pages. The home page of your website is a great place to start, since it likely has the most SEO authority. However, don't stop there. Look for deeper pages in your website that are important and optimize the titles for those pages too. For most businesses, the traffic potential of these deep pages when added up is significant.

TIPS FROM THE TRENCHES FOR PAGE TITLES

Here are four tips on writing great page titles:

1. Put your most important keywords in your Page Title. Too many websites fail to use the power of the Page Title in helping with their SEO. This is such an easy win. Make sure your Page Titles contain your most important keywords.

2. Earlier words in the Page Title carry more weight than later words, so put your most important words first. For example, instead of "User Friendly Inventory Management Software," try

FIGURE 6.2   Screen Shot of Page Title on Google

"Inventory Management Software That's User Friendly." The term "inventory management" is probably more important (from a search ranking perspective) than "user friendly."

3. Don't forget the humans! The goal is not just to rank for your important keywords, but to actually have visitors click through to your website. If your Page Title sounds like nonsense, written more for a computer than for a human, people are unlikely to click on it. Make sure your Page Title tag is something that users will want to click on when they see it in the search results.

4. When picking the Page Title tag for your home page, consider putting your company name at the end of the title. This allows your most important keywords to have more weight.

Adding an Effective Description

Similar to the page title, the meta description tag is information *about* a web page. It is usually a brief summary of what a user can expect to see on a page. Also like the page title, the meta description is included in special HTML code in the page and doesn't show up in the browser like the rest of the content.

From an SEO perspective, the meta description doesn't impact search rankings in any of the major search engines. So, including your keywords in the meta description will not help your rankings. However, the meta description is important because although the engines don't use it for rankings, they do often use it within the search results page. The description (or a portion thereof) is often included below the page title. By writing a compelling and accurate description for the page, you are more likely to get clicks from web users. (See Figure 6.3.)

Here are three tips for writing your page descriptions:

1. Keep them short (one to two sentences) and no more than 160 characters, because Google truncates long descriptions.

2. Every page should have a unique description (just like it should have a unique page title).

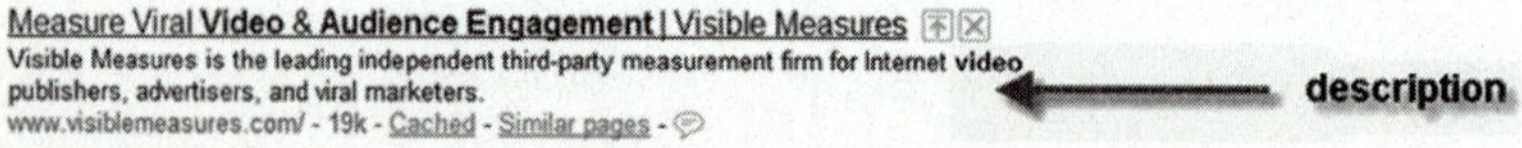

Figure 6.3   Page Description in Search Results

3. Use your keywords in your description. Google will often show the matching keywords from the search query as **bold** in the description. Having your keywords shown in this way increases the chances that users will click on your link in the results.

Optimizing URLs

Every publicly accessible resource on the Internet has a unique URL which is basically the Internet address of the page. (In case you were wondering, URL stands for "Uniform Resource Locator.")

Here are some sample URLs:

http://en.wikipedia.org/wiki/Url

www.hubspot.com/cmos-guide-to-brand-journalism

Most modern content management systems will let you customize the URLs for your web pages. You should take advantage of this feature and optimize your URLs from an SEO perspective. When Google crawls a web page, it looks at the URL as one of the factors it considers to determine the relevance of a web page for a given keyword. In the HubSpot example above, note that both the words "CMO" and "brand" are in the URL. If a user is searching on Google for the term "CMO branding guide," this keyword-rich URL sends a subtle signal to Google that this is likely what the page is about, in addition to looking at other things like the page title and content. Second, when users link to your website, they often just copy/paste the URL into their web pages and do not go to the trouble of specifying the anchor text. In these cases, the URL often *becomes* the anchor text. If you have your target keywords in the URL itself, you'll have a higher chance of getting anchor text with those keywords when people link to your page.

Domain Names and SEO

A topic that comes up frequently when discussing URLs is the importance of the domain name. The domain name is that part of the URL that is shared by all other pages on the site (for example, hubspot.com and inbound.org are both domain names). Since the domain name is part of *all* URLs on a given website, it is often useful to have a keyword contained within your domain name. The reason is simple, since all of your URLs contain your domain name, any keywords that are in your domain name automatically become part of all of your URLs. This is why keyword-rich domain names have long been so popular. The question is, should you change your domain name so that it contains one or more of your most important keywords? It depends. For a business website, the domain name should likely match the name of the business. If the business happens to contain a descriptive keyword, then you're fine. If not, it's unlikely that you want to change the name of the website and the business, simply to get a keyword-rich domain. Further, if you do decide to change your domain name, it will take some time and effort to reclaim any SEO authority you have built on the old domain name. Tread lightly here. We've gone through this process several times and it always has its challenges.

If you do want to use a domain name that has one or more keywords in it (which may be the case if you're a startup and have not decided on a business name yet), keep these points in mind: The best domain names are those that are relatively short, unambiguously clear, and memorable. If you're running a business, you want to focus only on .com domain names. Though there are other top-level domains, such as .net, .biz, .info, and others, the .com extension is the de facto standard for businesses. A noteworthy exception is international domains such as .ca (Canada), .in (India), and others, which are common for businesses within their respective countries.

The pool of unregistered, high-quality .com domain names with specific keywords is very limited. There's now an after-market for domain names, where you can acquire domain names that have been previously registered by someone else. If you're looking for a very high-quality domain name, you're likely going to have to pay more than just the registration fee. Prices for domain names can vary significantly from hundreds of dollars to hundreds of thousands of dollars. If you're starting a new business and traffic from search engines is extremely critical, you should consider creating your business name *around* a premium, high-quality domain name. Note however that over the years, Google has updated its search algorithm to reduce the impact of having keywords in a domain name. There was a time when an "exact match" domain (where the domain name matched exactly a specific search phrase) was an effective way to rise to the top of the search results. That is no longer the case. So, if you're investing in a premium domain name, do it for the brand value and the user experience—not search engine rankings.

PAGE CONTENT

So far, we've talked about the page title and the page meta description. Both of these are stored in a separate part of the web page because they describe the page. Now, let's discuss the page content itself, the body of the page. There are several considerations to keep in mind here too, from an SEO perspective.

HEADINGS

When creating a web page, you can put headings in the page content. Much like the headings in a book or newspaper article, a heading in a web page is used to help organize information and to help make the content easier to read. When a visitor is scanning through an article, the headings act as visual cues as to what she might expect to see. For example, an article in the Sunday paper about the most popular things to do in town might have subheadings such as "Museums," "Theatre," "Restaurants," and "Sporting Events." As you scan through this article, your eyes would quickly see the subheadings and know what you'd expect to find in the article. Google does something similar when reading your website. It looks at the headings in the page to determine what the page is about. This is why you should include your important keywords in the headings. When Google finds headings in your web page, it sees keywords in these headings as a signal that these words are important.

Just because some words look like a heading to people doesn't mean they look that way to Google. You must "tag" words on your pages so they look like headings to the search engines.

TIPS FROM THE TRENCHES FOR HEADINGS

Follow these three tips for writing headings:

1. Use your important keywords in your heading.
2. Keep headings as short as possible so keywords get maximum weight (same principle as in the page title and URL).
3. Use a single h1 header on each page, and use multiple h2 and h3 headers.

IMAGES

Many web pages also include images. Images are a great way to illustrate a point and make content more attractive and appealing.

FIGURE 6.4   Screen Shot of Multiple Images on a Web Page

This is particularly true for long pieces of content with a lot of text. From an SEO perspective, one important thing to understand is that Google can't really "see" images, or any text that's in the image. For example, in Figure 6.4, though the words "Wall Street Journal" exist, they're part of a larger image so Google wouldn't really see those words.

If your web page content consists primarily of images that have text on them, Google will not really be able to interpret the text embedded in those images. As such, they're not signaling to Google as to what your website is about. A quick tip to determine whether certain text on a page is an image: Try to highlight the text with your mouse, as if you were going to copy/paste it. If you can't highlight the text, chances are it's an image and Google can't see it. To help with this, all important images on your web page should include what is known as an "alt" attribute. This is a special code that allows you to describe an image with text in a way that Google can see it. Also, like the URL of your web pages, the URL of your important images should contain your keywords.

Off-Page SEO: The Power of Inbound Links

Although the on-page SEO factors we discussed earlier are important and relatively easy to do, to make any significant improvement in rankings for your keywords you're going to need to address off-page factors as well. Off-page factors are those that are not on the pages you control but on other web pages. The most important off-page factor is inbound links. An inbound link is a link on another web page that points to your page. As discussed earlier, Google places a great deal of emphasis on the authority of a web page in determining search rankings. Authority is calculated based on the number of inbound links to your web page, and the authority of those pages linking to you.

The most effective way to get inbound links is by creating *remark-able* content that is useful and interesting. And, getting inbound links is the most effective way to get better rankings in Google.

REQUESTING LINKS FROM OTHERS

One way to get links from other people is to contact them and request that they link to your site. This is often done through an e-mail to the website owner for a site that you'd like to get a link from. Although this can work in some situations, we're not big fans of the link-requesting model. It's hard to get great, high-quality links by requesting them from other people who don't know you. Like most site owners, we get requests for links all the time. We treat these link requests like spam messages—we delete them. Having said that, if you've created some exceptionally good content that you think would be beneficial to the readers of a particular site or blog, it is fine to reach out to them. When reaching out to bloggers or site owners, make sure the e-mail is highly personalized. Demonstrate that you read their site and understand their audience. Send a link to the content you think would be relevant for them. Usually, this is not your home page, but a deeper page, like a blog article. Finally, don't explicitly ask for a link. You're basically sharing information that you think they might find useful. If they like it and think it would be interesting to their audiences, they might link to it.

MEASURING THE VALUE OF INBOUND LINKS

With the proliferation of blogs and the comments left on those blogs, Google ran into an issue. Most blog comments allow the commenter to enter a URL that links back to a web page of their choice—usually the comment author's blog or company website. The problem was that this feature allowed any user to create an inbound link for themselves on any website that allowed user-submitted content, making life difficult for Google. The search engine could not distinguish legitimate inbound links, which were seen as an endorsement, and which could be used as a signal of quality for the page being linked to, and potentially low-quality links that the website owner didn't really create. To solve this, the "no-follow" attribute was created for links.

JOE'S SEO CONSULTANT ADVISES HIM TO DO SOME LINK ~~BEGGING~~ BUILDING.

The no-follow attribute is information within the source code for a page that can be included on a link. When Google sees a link that is marked as a no-follow, it treats this as a signal that the site owner does not wish to pass SEO credit to the target page. Though users can still click on the link (it looks and behaves like any other link), it does not help the page being linked to from an SEO perspective. Today, most blogs automatically mark all links left within comments as no-follow. In fact, most software that allows user-generated content (content created by the general public, not by the site owner) will mark the links within this content to be no-follow.

It's important to recognize that spending lots of time creating content on other people's websites with the sole purpose of getting SEO value doesn't work very well. Most of those links will be no-follow and, as such, will not pass SEO credit.

So, how much is a given link worth from an SEO perspective? Many factors go into determining how much SEO authority you will receive from a given inbound link.

Factors That Affect Link Value

There are four factors that affect link value:

1. The authority of the page that the link is on. The higher the authority of the page, the more of this authority it can pass on to your web page.
2. Whether the link is a no-follow or a do-follow as discussed above.
3. The number of other links on the page linking to you. The more links that are on that page, the less SEO credit each link passes.
4. The anchor text of the link. This is the text that the user sees on the page and that is clickable. By default, anchor text shows up as underlined on most web pages. Links that have your desired keywords in the anchor text are the most valuable to you in terms of ranking for those keywords.

Black Hat SEO: How to Get Your Site Banned by Google

The terms "black hat" and "white hat" were derived from old western movies where the bad guys generally wore black hats and the good guys wore white hats. SEO experts constantly debate as to what practices are considered white hat versus black hat. In our mind, the big difference is that white-hat SEO *helps* Google deliver quality results to users by working within existing guidelines. On the other hand, black-hat SEO involves exploiting current limitations in Google's software to try and trick it into ranking a particular web page that would normally not have ranked.

Whatever you call them, you should avoid SEO practices that rely on tricking Google and distorting search results. Here's our rule of thumb: If a given technique is not improving the experience for a user, and it can be detected by a human doing a manual review, then it's probably a bad idea. It's safe to assume that if you try to exploit a hole in the Google software today, your advantage is going to be temporary. More importantly, you carry a significant risk of having your website penalized or banned completely from Google. The risk is not worth the reward.

Here are the techniques you should stay away from when optimizing your site for Google.

Link Farms

There's general consensus that one of the strongest influences on search rankings is the number and quality of inbound links to a web page. A link farm is a group of websites created for the primary purpose of creating a high number of links to a given web page. These websites are not real, and the links on them are not genuine signals of quality. They are often generated automatically by computers and their content is of minimal, if any, value.

Automated Content Generation/Duplication

Search engines like content. They particularly like frequently updated content. Unfortunately, creating unique content takes time and energy. In order to try to trigger search engine spiders to index more pages from a website and do so more frequently, some may try to autogenerate content or scrape content from other sites and republish it. This technique often goes hand-in-hand with link farms. That's because if you're creating thousands of sites, you need *some* content to put on them. Google has gotten very good at determining natural content versus content that is computer-generated gibberish with no value. As for duplicating content on other websites without permission, this is not only penalized by Google, it is often a violation of copyright laws.

Keyword Stuffing

This practice involves overpopulating certain portions of a web page with a set of keywords in the hope that it will increase the chances that Google will rank the page for that keyword. Search engines caught on to this trick years ago, and it's no longer effective. Of course, this doesn't keep people from trying it.

Cloaking

This tactic involves delivering *different* website content to Google's search spider than what is delivered to human users. The usual motivation for this is to send the search engine crawlers content for ranking on a certain term—but send different content to real users. It's pretty easy for the search engines to detect this. If you're suspected of using cloaking, it's easy for someone (like a Google employee) to simply visit your website as a human and check if you're cloaking. This technique, when discovered, is one of the most reliable ways to get a site banned.

Hidden Text

This technique hides text on the web page. The idea is to include text so only Google can see it, but humans cannot. The simplest example is some variation of white text on a white background. This combination is not easily visible to human users, but from a computer's perspective, the content still exists. This technique is a bit harder for Google to detect, but not by any means impossible.

Doorway/Gateway Pages

This practice is similar to the cloaking technique. Instead of dynamically delivering different content to Google, a doorway page involves getting a given page to rank well in Google, but then redirecting human users to a different page. Clearly, this is not in the interests of end users, as they don't get the content they would have expected.

It's not smart to try to outsmart Google engineers. Just about all of these questionable tactics presume that the search engines will not detect them and are based on exploiting *currently presumed* (and perhaps even nonexistent) limitations of search engine algorithms. We'd argue that Google as a company is pretty smart and spends considerable resources updating its algorithm. An Internet strategy that's predicated on outsmarting Google is not a smart one.

For most marketers, the time and energy spent on trying to take these shortcuts is much better invested in improving the company website and content so that it *deserves* to be ranked highly, and *helping* the search engines discover this content for the benefit of users. Working *with* search engines instead of trying to *exploit* them is the only approach to SEO that works in the long-term.

The Dangers of PPC

We've talked a fair amount about organic rankings and how to effectively approach SEO. But, we haven't spent a lot of time talking about paid search via PPC.

PPC advertising has proven to be an effective way for many marketers to drive targeted traffic to their websites. However, there's long-term risk in becoming too reliant on PPC for traffic. The problem is that because PPC programs like Google's AdWords act as a real-time auction, it is possible for the cost per click (CPC) to rise unexpectedly.

Let's look at a concrete example of this. Say you're buying clicks for "wedding caterers San Francisco" and you're paying about $2.50 a click. You've analyzed the data and have determined that at this price, the clicks are worth it because the value of the leads generated from these clicks exceeds the cost. Now, things are going along just fine and then one morning, you find that your CPC has risen to over $3.00, a 20 percent increase. This can happen for a variety of reasons, but the most common is that there is suddenly new competition that is interested in that same word, and they're willing to pay more. Even if you're a PPC expert, there's little you can do to prevent others bidding up the price. You are vulnerable because the price changes constantly based on competition. Your prices can spike and do so very quickly. Contrast this to how SEO works. If you make an investment in ranking for your top keywords in the organic listings, it is much less likely that a new market entrant that doesn't understand the business is going to be able to displace you quickly and take away the traffic you are getting. Organic listings are usually not achieved by new entrants that are just getting started. Even throwing money at it (as they can do in PPC) doesn't work very well. And, even if this new competitor does ultimately beat you in the organic rankings, it will likely happen over time. You can watch the rankings for your top keywords and see if competitors are gaining ground.

So, our advice is to appropriately balance your investment in PPC and SEO. In the early days of building web traffic, it might be necessary to buy traffic. Or, you might be running a short campaign to collect valuable data about which keywords work. However, over time, you should work towards establishing your organic rankings. This investment has a better rate of return in the long-term and is much more defensible.

Tracking Your Progress

Tracking your progress in terms of rankings is an important part of SEO—and it's relatively easy.

Use the free Website Grader (grader.com) tool and create a custom report for your website. It will give you a lot of useful information, find problems, and give you suggestions to fix them. Make a note of what your score is, follow the suggestions, and regularly monitor your grade over time. website Grader looks at several different factors and gives you a higher-level view of how your website is doing.

One of the data points you should check is how many of your site's pages are in the Google index. If the number of indexed pages seems lower than you expect (or zero), there's likely some problem with your site architecture and Google is not seeing all of your web pages.

Monitor the number of inbound links you are getting to your website. As we've discussed earlier, your Google rankings depend a lot on the number and quality of links you are getting. You should be working to get this number higher and higher.

Track a list of your favorite keywords (those that have the right mix of relevance, high search volume, and low difficulty) and see how your rankings are doing. You'll find that you do better for some words than others. Start looking for patterns. Pay particular attention to which web pages on your site are starting to rank. These pages are important assets because Google is sending you a message (by ranking those pages) that they are gaining authority.

Most importantly, track your *actual* results. How many visitors are coming to your website through organic search? How many became leads? For bonus points, implement a closed-loop reporting system and track how many of these leads converted into customers. (Closed loop means you track a new customer from initial inquiry to closed sale.)

Inbound in Action: LinkedIn "Elite"

Inbound isn't just about attracting a new audience. It's also about keeping your current audience actively engaged. LinkedIn understands this need as well as any organization.

The company needed to find ways to remind its members to return to LinkedIn—to augment their profiles, discover a presentation on newly acquired SlideShare, or stumble upon a job (better still, an advertisement for a job)—regularly, not just when they are conducting an active employment search. But what could it offer that would draw a meaningful number of its members back to the social network?

Rather than produce a piece of content or develop an online tool, the company provided a more elemental value: an ego stroke.

When LinkedIn logged its 200 millionth member, instead of issuing a self-congratulatory press release, it congratulated its most influential members. The company e-mailed a note to the previous year's top 1, 5, and 10 percent most-viewed profiles. The message thanked those members for playing a "unique part" in the LinkedIn community.

The value of the message was multifold. It not only reminded its most popular members to re-engage with LinkedIn, but it also motivated them to share their accomplishment across various social networks, drawing in their circles of influence.

It might have only been a simple e-mail, but the right message at the right time to the right audience can be a powerful inbound lure.

To Do

1. Run your website through grader.com. Follow the suggestions.
2. Discover which of your pages are the most powerful.
3. Optimize the page titles of your most important pages (like your home page).
4. _____
5. _____
6. _____
7. _____

Chapter 7

Get Found in Social Media

Social media is all the rage. We'll bet that not a week (or perhaps even a day) goes by when you're not having a colleague connect with you on LinkedIn, receiving a friend request on Facebook, or hearing about Twitter on TV. What is social media? The all-knowing Wikipedia defines social media as "Internet-based tools for sharing and discussing information among human beings." That's not a bad definition. We'd simplify it and say that social media is about people connecting, interacting, and sharing online.

Why should you care about social media? The answer is the same as why you should care about Google—because it provides a great way to reach and engage potential customers. As is the case with Google, more of your potential customers hang out at the social media watering holes, so this is where you need to hang out, too, if you want to engage with them.

You can find a variety of social media sites on the web today. These include social networking (such as Facebook, Twitter, and LinkedIn), social news sites (like reddit), and social bookmarking/discovery sites (like StumbleUpon). Each has its different uses, but most share the ability to create a user profile, connect to others on the site, and interact and share information with the network's community of people.

Creating an Effective Online Profile

In the rest of this chapter, we look at specific social media websites and how you can leverage them, but before we do that, let's look at one aspect that's common to most of these sites: the user profile. A profile often consists of your username, avatar image, bio/summary, and web links. As you start building a social media presence, it's helpful to spend a little bit of time thinking about how you approach building your professional brand in social media.

PICKING A USERNAME

For many of the social media sites (e.g., LinkedIn and Facebook), you don't invent a new username for yourself—you access the site *as yourself*. In fact, creating a fictitious person or a persona is in violation of the terms of service of these sites and is likely to get you kicked off. But not all sites operate this way. Sites like StumbleUpon and Twitter allow you to create any username you want. Based on your goals, different approaches to a username might make sense. If you're reading this book, we'll assume that you're a business person trying to expand marketing reach for a product or service. In that case, we have several tips for usernames:

1. Wherever possible, use your real name for your username. For example, we use @bhalligan and @dharmesh for our primary Twitter accounts. (We also have @hubspot for our business.)
2. Make your username simple and clean. Stay away from user-names that play clever games (e.g., using the number "3" as a backwards letter "E").
3. Don't include numerals in your username. Not only is this reminiscent of a bygone era ("Hi, I'm John4382 on AOL!"), there's a chance that people will think your account is a bit spammy.
4. Pick a name that's available on all or most of the major social sites so that you can have a consistent name across as many sites as possible. If you have a common name, this may be difficult, but try your best. The goal is to build your online brand so people start recognizing you.

PICKING AN ONLINE AVATAR/PROFILE IMAGE

In addition to your username, all of the social media sites allow you to upload a small image associated with your account. This image shows up with your profile, and often is attached to comments and other contributions you make on the site. Pick a nice photo of yourself and make sure it's the right dimensions when you upload it. Try a couple of variations. If you lack the technical skills to resize and retouch photos, get a friend or family member to help. The profile image is an important part of your online identity and it's not that hard to get it right. Use the same image across all of your social media profiles. If you're setting up social media accounts for your business, your avatar image should be some variation of your logo. Think of your profile image as part of your overall brand (because it is). Try for something that is distinctive and memorable. Be consistent.

Bio/Summary

Social media sites usually let you tell the world about yourself with a short, one- or two-sentence description. Don't skip this step! Many people in social media will read your bio to determine if they're interested in hearing what you have to say. A missing bio rarely instills confidence and people are likely to just skip by you, so it pays to spend the time to write a brief but compelling bio. When writing your bio, we advise focusing on the people with whom you're interested in connecting. Though some of them may care that you're a dog lover or wine expert, they're more likely interested in knowing your area of business expertise and what they can expect to gain from being connected with you. Of course, there's nothing wrong with instilling some personality in your bio, just be interesting and relevant.

Website Links

Social media sites often allow you to enter one or more links to websites where people can learn more about you or your company. Common approaches include linking to your blog (if you have one) or to your business website. Unfortunately, these links generate little (if any) SEO value. They're usually no-follow links (which don't pass SEO credit). However, they can still generate traffic to your desired website, so you should take advantage of them.

Getting Fans on Facebook

Facebook is one of the largest and most active social networking sites on the Internet. As of this writing, some quick stats on Facebook:

♦ More than 1.1 billion active users (yes, that's billion with a "b").
♦ Over 700 million users log in every day.
♦ Fastest-growing demographic is people aged 45–54.

This last statistic is particularly interesting because although Facebook started as a website for college students, it has grown well beyond that and is no longer a website just for college students to hang out on. It's now a widespread application used by millions of people of all ages.

You may be wondering what the advantage is of having a presence on a social media site like Facebook when your business already has a regular website. The answer is *reach*. You want your message and story to reach as many people as possible. To maximize your reach, you need to have a presence where people are hanging out and increasingly they're hanging out on Facebook.

Creating a business page on Facebook is easy and free. Once created, the page can be branded with your company's logo and customized to include information about your business and a link back to your main website. Users on Facebook can then become "fans" of your business page by "liking" it. In addition to providing a page that has basic information about your organization, Facebook allows a multitude of other features that help better engage your community. These include discussion forums, photos, videos, testimonials, and hundreds of other features created by third-party developers. These interactive features truly make Facebook a vibrant community where like-minded individuals can interact and share.

What makes Facebook's reach particularly powerful is its *viral* aspect. When individual users join your community on Facebook, their friends see an update in their Facebook home pages. This leads to more users joining your community, causing more people to be exposed to your business, and so on. By leveraging this social aspect of Facebook, businesses have a chance to reach a large group of people.

CREATING A FACEBOOK BUSINESS PAGE

All Facebook users have a personal page where they can post information about themselves, post status updates that others will see, and share information, such as photos and links. In addition to your personal page, you should create a separate page for your business.

If you don't yet have a personal account on Facebook, create it *first*. You should not create a standard user account for a business. This is in violation of Facebook's terms of service, and you will be at risk of having your account terminated.

To create a business page, you must first be logged in with your personal account (only logged-in users can create fan pages). Once you're logged in, visit the following URL: www.facebook.com/pages/create.php.

The first step in creating your page is to determine which category it falls into. You can choose from many choices organized by Local, Brand/Product/Organization, and Artist/Band/Public Figure. Pick the one that fits best.

Once you've created a business page for your company, you'll need to spend some time promoting it. Here are a few ways you can do that:

1. Post a link to your business page from your personal profile. You can do this by clicking the "share" button when viewing your business page.
2. Promote your new Facebook business page within your existing channels (your company website, your blog, your e-mail newsletter, your LinkedIn profile, etc.).
3. Buy social ads on Facebook. Facebook shows these ads to targeted users within various locations on the site.

Pro tip: To make it easy for potential customers to visit and remember the location of your Facebook page, create a subdomain (facebook.yourcompany.com) on your main domain that sends users to your Facebook business page. It's free and takes just a few minutes for whoever is managing your domain configuration. You should also customize the URL for your Facebook business page. This way, users can access the page with a URL that looks like http://facebook.com/yourcompany instead of the ugly and indecipherable default URL that Facebook provides.

Learning from Facebook Ads

Facebook allows businesses to advertise their business pages (or any other web page) within Facebook. These ads are shown to specific Facebook users in various parts of the site.

Even if you're not planning to buy Facebook social ads, it's worth taking the first step as if you're launching an ad. Facebook's ad tool allows you to specify demographics such as age and gender—which is a great way to get a rough sense of how many Facebook users fit your target market. Figure 7.1 shows a sample demographic for "marketing": 47,260 people over the age of 25 in the United States have specified the word "marketing" somewhere in their profile. Try running this tool for your own industry and see how many users you can find. This is particularly helpful if you're a local business focused on a specific geographic area, as Facebook allows targeting by location, as well.

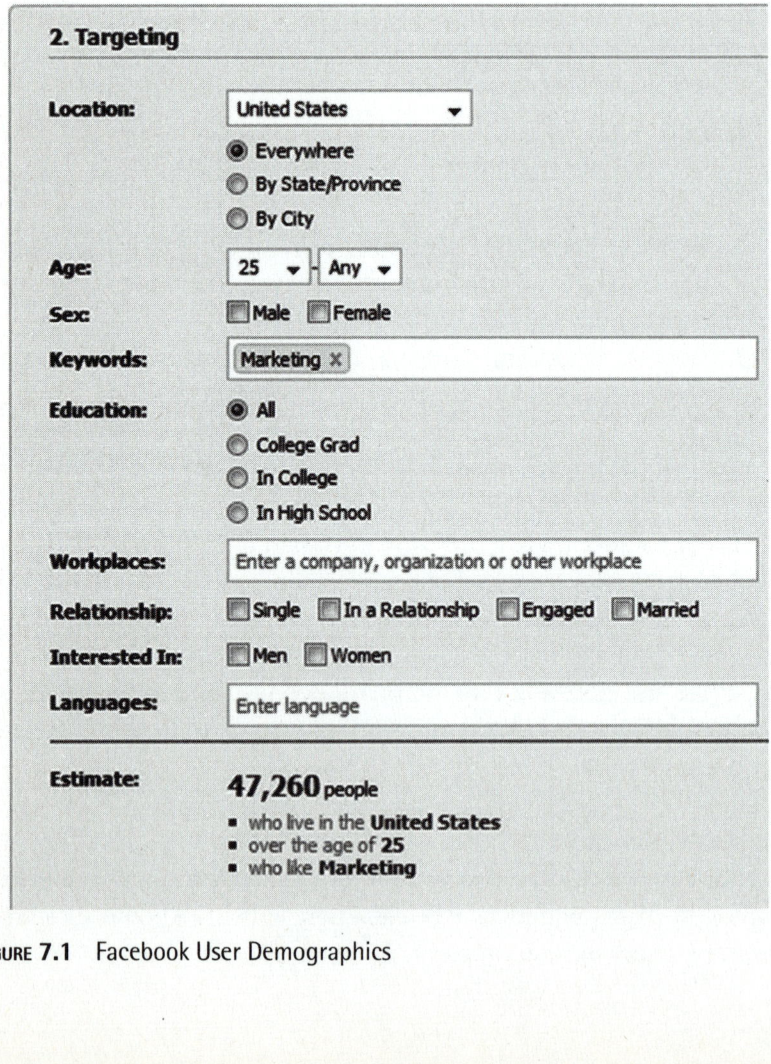

2. Targeting

Location: United States ▾
- ◉ Everywhere
- ○ By State/Province
- ○ By City

Age: 25 ▾ – Any ▾

Sex: ☐ Male ☐ Female

Keywords: Marketing ×

Education:
- ◉ All
- ○ College Grad
- ○ In College
- ○ In High School

Workplaces: Enter a company, organization or other workplace

Relationship: ☐ Single ☐ In a Relationship ☐ Engaged ☐ Married

Interested In: ☐ Men ☐ Women

Languages: Enter language

Estimate: **47,260** people
- who live in the **United States**
- over the age of **25**
- who like **Marketing**

FIGURE 7.1   Facebook User Demographics

Getting started on Facebook is easy, but it requires a certain amount of ongoing attention to achieve maximum value, as users expect to see fresh information on the site. You should plan to have someone in your company accountable for updating the site and participating in the conversations regularly. Devoting time to fostering a social networking page may be a bit of a challenge for small businesses with limited resources, but it's a worthwhile investment. Sites like Facebook are large enough and growing quickly enough that they should not be ignored. Having a presence on a social networking site is swiftly becoming as important as having a website. The social media sites are, in a sense, an extension of a traditional website. Facebook's functionality, viral nature, and large user base makes it an ideal marketing platform for many different types of organizations.

Tips from the Trenches

Here are three important tips:

1. Don't create a fake account. Be genuine.
2. Check the insights feature of the Facebook pages regularly to see how well your business page is doing.
3. Link to your Facebook page from your business website and from other online materials. Build reach within your community.

Creating Connections on LinkedIn

If you're a business professional, there's a good chance that you've heard of LinkedIn and have already registered as a user. LinkedIn is a website for professional social networking; the average age of users on the site is 41. Unlike other social networks such as Myspace and Facebook, which focus on a broad set of users, LinkedIn is all about business. As we write this, it has amassed over 277 million users. The LinkedIn basics are similar to Facebook. You register for an account and build out your profile including a brief summary or bio, employment history, and academic credentials. In the case of LinkedIn, this is most often work colleagues. Also similar to Facebook, you can create a *company page* on LinkedIn.

Like most social networks, LinkedIn also allows you to connect to others. This information about millions of people, including their connections, is what makes LinkedIn such a powerful tool. Let's say you're looking for a new position as a VP of Marketing at a specific organization. LinkedIn allows you to search its database and find people at that company whom you are somehow connected to. What makes this particularly useful is that you don't have to be *directly* connected to these individuals, as LinkedIn finds a path between you and those with whom you want to connect. For example, let's say you're trying to connect to the CEO of a specific company. You don't actually know the CEO, but someone in your immediate list of connections does—in fact, a colleague of yours from a prior job is now reporting directly to this CEO. LinkedIn allows you to request a virtual introduction through one or more intermediate connections. This is a powerful way to leverage LinkedIn's social network to connect with people for mutual interest and gain.

BUILDING A LINKEDIN GROUP

Groups are a very powerful feature of the LinkedIn system. A LinkedIn Group is essentially an online community of people interested in a particular topic (whatever the focus of the group is). There are currently over 1.9 million different Groups on LinkedIn covering a wide range of topics. We have a Group, Inbound Marketers, which happens to be one of the largest groups on LinkedIn with over 100,000 members.

Starting a Group is quick, easy, and free. If you have not already done so, determine if a Group already exists that focuses on your industry or area of interest. To do this, you can use the Groups search feature by clicking the dropdown arrow next to the "Search People" field in the top right corner of the application (see Figure 7.2). Select "Search Groups" from the list of available searches and then enter some keywords that describe the kinds of groups you're looking for.

Figure 7.3 shows the results from a sample search for "small business." (Notice when you do your own search that the "OnStartups" group is the number one result with 59,459 members. Dharmesh is the creator of this Group and of the 250,000+ Groups, it is one of the top five largest.)

Notice when you do your own search for the term "startups," the OnStartups group is the #1 result with 414,000 members. Dharmesh is

FIGURE 7.2 Clicking "Search People"

the creator of this group, and of the 2 million groups on LinkedIn, it is one of the largest. When creating your Group, pick a name that describes your topic of interest *and* is something that people will potentially want to be a member of. A convenient way to think of great Group names is to try to complete this sentence:

I am a proud member of _____.

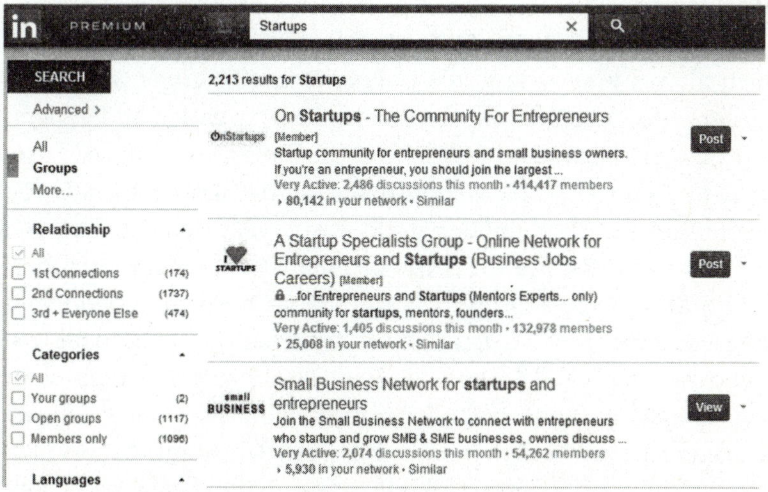

FIGURE 7.3 Example of LinkedIn Search Results for "Small Business"

There's a reason this is important. When people join your group, by default, a small logo/badge for your group shows up on that user's personal profile. The clearer it is who your group is for and why someone might want to be a member, the more likely they are to join. For example, one of the groups we've created is named "Inbound Marketers." For the people in our target market (professional marketers), it's easy to see how they'd want to have a badge on their profiles that says "Inbound Marketers."

When writing the description of your Group, make sure to include your most important keywords. This way, when people use the LinkedIn search feature to find Groups of interest, yours is more likely to show up. The Group search function in LinkedIn is much simpler than Google's. The way it currently works is that all Groups containing the search term in their title or description are shown in descending order of size (number of members). As with many other online channels, size counts. You want to attract as many members to your Group as possible.

Promote your Group through your available channels. Put it in your e-mail signature. Highlight it on your website. Write a blog article about it. Send it out in your next quarterly newsletter. Post discussions from your Group to Twitter. The name of the game is to get people to join your Group. The more people that join, the more people will see your Group's badge on other people's user profiles. The more people that see your badge, the more people join. This creates what is known as a "virtuous cycle"—success leads to more success.

Similar to Facebook, LinkedIn also has an advertising product which allows you to buy ads online. You can target ads based on user attributes such as company size, industry, gender, and geography. Ads can be purchased on a CPM basis (how many people will the ad be shown to) or on a CPC basis (how many people click on the ads). Based on your budget, ads might be a good way to get some initial traction for your Group, which in turn helps you attract even more members.

Once you have a Group with members, be sure to build value in being a member of it. First, and most importantly, LinkedIn allows you to send an e-mail to all Group members. This is very easy to do since the e-mail is sent from the LinkedIn.com domain. As a result, this e-mail message has a pretty high deliverability rate (meaning it's less likely to get caught in spam filters). LinkedIn's Group messaging capability is a great way to update the Group and share information. As is the case with any mass communication mechanism, you should be thoughtful as to how often you send messages and what you write in the messages. You don't want to send something too frequently or be selling too hard, at the risk of seeming spammy. Next, post messages to the discussion area of your Group. Although this capability is available to all the Group members, as the administrator, you'll have the ability to "pin" your particular posts to the discussion forum so that they always show up at the top and don't scroll off. This way, you get more prominent placement for your discussions and they're more likely to be seen.

Gathering Followers on Twitter

Twitter has quickly become a worldwide phenomenon with millions of current users and tens of thousands of new users joining every day. Although Twitter is described in different ways, the most common description is that Twitter is a microblogging platform. If you're wondering what a microblog is, the answer is simple: you post "articles" (just like a blog), but each "article" is a maximum of 140 characters long. Users on Twitter post these short updates, which are called "tweets." You can post tweets from the Twitter website, a mobile device, or any number of custom applications built by third parties. Who sees these tweets? By default, they're posted publicly (so anyone can see them). In practice, they're most often noticed by others users who are *following* the person posting the tweet (see Figure 7.4).

Early uses of Twitter were basically akin to the status updates feature in Facebook. Twitter users posted quick updates, which

FIGURE 7.4   Screen Shot for Posting on Twitter

answered the question the Twitter website asked: "What are you doing?" The result was a seemingly endless stream of short updates about what people were doing in their regular lives: where they were having lunch, what movie they were going to see, and just about anything else. As Twitter use evolved, the types of messages began to be more diverse. Instead of answering the "what are you doing" question, more people began posting information, links, and reactions to this information and to world events as they happened in real time. Conversations started to take place. Today, Twitter is used in many different ways by a variety of people and age groups.

Our first reaction to Twitter when we encountered it was the same reaction many people have: "How is this useful? Why do I care what other people are having for lunch? How is this going to help me grow my business?" Like many busy business people, we initially dismissed Twitter because it seemed unlikely that a steady stream of tweets about the minutiae of daily existence could somehow help us market our business better. But, surprisingly, it works! We're now big believers in the usefulness of Twitter. Sure, there is still a relatively high volume of tweets that do little more than tell us what someone is having for lunch, but amongst these are conversations that we'd consider useful. People ask questions about products or services, customers post reviews, and conference attendees tweet live updates from a workshop or panel.

GETTING STARTED WITH TWITTER

If you don't yet have a Twitter account, your first step is to create one. Twitter has one of the simplest registration systems out there and it takes just a minute to get up and running. You must first decide whether you should create a username based on your name or the name of your company. We suggest making your primary account based on your name. But, we think you should also create an account for your business. Accounts are free, and even if you don't think you're going to need a Twitter account for your business, it doesn't hurt to go ahead and reserve the name before someone else does. Unlike domain names, registering a Twitter account is completely free.

Like most social media sites, Twitter lets you complete an online profile. We'd suggest that you go ahead and take a few minutes to complete your profile. This would include a photo, a link to your website, a short bio/summary of yourself, and your location. We've found that the more complete your profile is, the more likely it is that people will connect to you.

The next step is to post a few tweets. Don't be overly concerned about the quality of your tweets—you're not looking to win literary awards for your writing skills (which would be difficult to do in just 140 characters anyway). Share some useful information or insightful comment. In the early days of your Twitter use, things will be a bit frustrating, because until you build a base of followers, very few people will see your tweets and you'll feel like you're talking to yourself. That's okay. The goal of these initial tweets is to have some content in your Twitter account. You need this *before* you start reaching out and connecting to others and building a following. The kinds of people you likely want as followers are unlikely to follow you if they see that you have an empty Twitter account. They have no way of knowing whether your interests overlap with theirs and whether you're going to share things that they would find useful.

BUILDING A FOLLOWING

Like most social media sites, Twitter also has the concept of friends. Other users on Twitter can *follow* you. When they do this, your tweets are shown to them. Similarly, you can also follow other users and, as a result, see their tweets within your Twitter stream. Note that unlike Facebook, where a connection has to be reciprocal to count, Twitter allows one-way relationships. This means you can follow people, but they don't have to follow you back for you to see their tweets. In any case, if you want your tweets to be seen, you will need to build a following.

Once you have your Twitter account, begin seeking out other users who are relevant. You can do this in several ways. One is to use the built-in search feature in Twitter (http://search.twitter.com). Just type in keywords relevant to your industry and Twitter will show you tweets from users including those keywords. As you find people who are interesting and relevant, just follow them.

MONITORING YOUR BRAND AND INDUSTRY

Another good way to find people to follow is to use the search function on Twitter and search for your brand and the terms you associate with your industry. For example, if you sell HR software, you can search Twitter for "HR software." When you do, you will discover that a lot of people on Twitter are talking about this topic. You can then follow people interested in this area and engage in meaningful, helpful conversations. Also search for the name of your company to see what people are saying about your brand.

This is an activity you should do regularly in order to stay on top of your brand and to influence your marketplace.

THE TYRANNY OF TWITTER BOTS

Several online tools let you put Twitter on autopilot for various activities. For example, you can program one of these tools to automatically follow back anyone that follows you. Some even allow you to programatically follow hundreds or thousands of users. The motivation behind using these kinds of tools is to help you amass a large number of followers in a short amount of time. Personally, we don't agree with these approaches. Our argument is not one of high moral or ethical ground (though we could certainly make the case for that too, if we tried), but rather, such automated means do not help with your real goal as an inbound marketer—to build productive relationships. These bulk following activities are akin to showing up at a business networking event and judging your success by how many business cards you can hand out to as many random people as possible. Though you may certainly get some hits in terms of people who have actual interest in your company, the most probable outcome is that you have little activity and low results. What's worse, you risk putting yourself in a negative light to those who matter. Our advice: Stay away from robotic approaches to building relationships online. Social networks are about being *social* and building genuine relationships for mutual gain with other *people,* not automated software systems.

Gaining Reach from Google+

Google launched its social network service, Google+, in 2011. The site was seen as Google's answer to Facebook and has grown rapidly. Google+ claims to have about half as many users as Facebook and twice as many as Twitter.

Marketing guru and former Apple evangelist Guy Kawasaki has been a big fan of Google+ and a heavy user of the service. In his book, *APE: Author, Publisher, Entrepreneur*, Kawasaki says he and his partners like Google+ because "it enables us to write lengthy posts, embed pictures and video, and interact with people who share our passions."

If you don't have a blog, or if your blog has a small audience, Kawasaki recommends just using Google+ as your blogging platform instead. "It is much easier to generate traffic for a Google+ account than for a standalone blog because of the built-in sharing and liking features of the service," he writes. Kawasaki has even published a guide to using Google+, titled *What the Plus!*

CIRCLES

The core feature of Google+ is called Circles. You can arrange people into various Circles, using a simple drag-and-drop interface. This lets you send work-related material to people in your "Work" Circle, family photos to your "Friends" Circle, and so on. You can also choose to publish something to everyone. Circles also work as a way to filter what you see in your stream. If you choose a Circle you will see material only from people in that Circle.

Another important feature is Hangouts, a free video-conferencing feature that supports up to 10 people. Google+ also offers Hangouts on Air, which is basically a live stream of an event. Once it's over, you can share the Hangout via your Google+ page and your YouTube channel. It's a free alternative to premium webinar software, but, being free, it lacks much of the scheduling and integration features that more established webinar providers offer.

GOOGLE+ FOR BUSINESS

You can and should create a Google+ page for your business. It's easy to do and will help your business show up on the web.

Customers can quickly get information about your company, like your hours of operation, address, phone number, and directions.

Also, verified information about your business will show up in Google Maps. If you have a YouTube channel, you can link it to your Google+ page.

Google has created a "Partner Playbook" that you will find useful. It's at the following URL:

http://services.google.com/fh/files/misc/googleplus-partner-play book-may13.pdf

Here are five steps that will help you get going on Google+.

1. Create a Google+ page. That's easy to do. You can start on this URL: www.google.com/+/business/.
2. Pick a category that your company falls under, such as "local business or place," or "product or brand."
3. Complete your profile. You want to make your page interesting and compelling. You'll want to include a link to your website and basic information about your business. If possible, you should also include photos and videos.
4. Claim your vanity URL. Google lets you claim a custom URL for your business. To get it, you sign in to Google+. Go to your profile, then the About tab, and under Links > Google+ URL, click "Get URL." Google generates the URL for you; you can't change what they give you.
5. Use Google+ buttons to gain more followers. If you put a "+1" button next to a piece of content on your website, people can click on that button to share your content on Google+ and recommend it on Google Search. The "+1" button is equivalent to Facebook's "Like" button.

We believe Google+ should be part of any social media strategy, alongside Facebook, Twitter, LinkedIn, and others. While it may be difficult to quantify the size of the audience you're reaching, the connection to Google and its search engine alone are reason enough to invest time in building a Google+ presence.

Being Discovered with StumbleUpon

StumbleUpon is another way to drive traffic to your best content through its network of over seven million registered users. Stumble-Upon is known as a social discovery site, as it helps you discover new content that you might like. Like most social media sites, it's free to use, and it's pretty easy to get started. Your first step is to register and create

StumbleUpon Toolbar

FIGURE 7.5   Screen Shot of StumbleUpon Toolbar

an account, at which point you indicate your areas of interest from over 100 different topic areas. You then download and install the Stumble-Upon toolbar for your browser. Once installed, the toolbar shows up right within your browser (see Figure 7.5) and on the toolbar you'll find a number of buttons, the first of which is "Stumble!"

When you click on the "Stumble!" button, you're taken automatically to a different web page from the one you're on. Which page you are taken to depends on several things, but primarily it depends on what you like and how popular the page is amongst the StumbleUpon user community. Once you're on the site, you can choose to up-vote it by clicking the "I Like It" button on the toolbar, or you can down-vote it by clicking the "Thumbs Down" button. As you might suspect, web pages that get more up-votes are shown to more users.

A web page that gets many StumbleUpon up-votes receives thousands of visitors. With StumbleUpon, you get gradually *more* traffic as you get more up-votes. This is good, because if you have moderately good content that just a few people up-vote, you'll still see a noticeable increase in traffic. The more positive votes you get, the more traffic you get. With StumbleUpon, traffic continues to be sent for a long time. We have popular articles from our blog submitted over two years ago that are *still* getting traffic from StumbleUpon!

MORE TIPS FROM THE TRENCHES

To use StumbleUpon successfully, use these tips:

1. Get to know all the basic categories available and select the ones that are the most relevant for your profile. This causes you to stumble into content that is more interesting to you.

2. When first starting, resist the temptation to submit your own content. Simply use StumbleUpon to find interesting content (that's what it's designed for). Up-vote things you like.

3. Begin making friends. Of particular interest to you are those people who were the initial stumblers who first found a web page that you found interesting. These users have shared interests with you and are more likely to up-vote your content.

4. Consider running a small paid advertising campaign on StumbleUpon (they charge about $0.05 per website visitor—but you can target based on their visitors' area of interest). This is often a cheap way to figure out whether a particular piece of content is likely to be a candidate for going viral on the web.

Getting Found on YouTube

YouTube was an extremely popular website even before Google acquired the company for $1.65 billion. Since then, its spectacular growth has continued and today it's one of the top 10 most-frequented sites on the Internet. Let's look at some quick numbers:

- ◆ YouTube gets more than 1 billion unique visitors each month.
- ◆ Over 6 billion hours of video are watched each month—that's almost half an hour, on average, for every person on Earth.

You should also note that YouTube is not just about hilarious videos of kittens doing crazy things (though that genre has proven to be a perennial favorite). You can find many different types of popular videos, including "How To," "Expert Interviews," recordings from conferences, and even funny commercials (but they have to be *really* funny).

The first step with getting started with YouTube is to set up an account for your business (e.g., www.youtube.com/yourcompany). When creating an account, you should pick a name that matches your business name because this name will also become the name of your YouTube channel. The next step is to start posting *remark*able videos (uploading video is pretty straightforward), which YouTube hosts for free—meaning you don't have to worry about bandwidth or storage costs.

We've outlined some ways you can create *remark*able videos.

Customer Stories

Record conversations with some of your best customers; have them share experiences and information that you think would be interesting to *future* customers. Though it's okay for your customers to talk about your business, don't force it. The goal is not to get a testimonial, but to have them share information that would be useful to others.

EXPERT INTERVIEWS

Find experts in your industry and record interviews with them. It is often easier to get people to agree to be interviewed in a podcast or video than to write a guest article for your blog.

HOW–TO VIDEOS

Videos are a great way to educate people, so it pays to build a library of short videos that your target audience would find interesting and helpful to their jobs.

The key to success on YouTube, as is the case with other inbound marketing channels we've talked about, is to produce *remark*able content that people will want to watch and share. Though you can certainly produce a video that's nothing more than a boring commercial for your product or service, it's unlikely to get many views (except maybe your mother, but even she is expecting more amusement from her web experience these days).

Recording short, high-quality videos can be done with most modern digital cameras. Even somewhat specialized videocams can be purchased relatively inexpensively. With a small amount of preparation and practice, you can, with relatively little expense and experience, record videos and share them with audiences on the web. Posting to YouTube is fast and easy and no extensive editing is required.

Once your video is available on YouTube, you'll need to drive traffic to it. This is done using the same channels you'd use to promote any of the content you produce—your website, your blog, and your social media accounts. One of the more useful features that YouTube provides is the ability to *embed* videos right within a web page, so that users don't even have to go to YouTube to view them. We use this feature to add our videos to our blog—in addition, we write content around the videos. By putting your YouTube videos in your blog articles, you're ensuring that at least your blog subscribers will see them. As you might expect, YouTube also has a search feature that allows people to find videos relating to specific topics. This works similarly to Google, but is much simpler. When optimizing your videos for a YouTube search, be sure to create a descriptive, attention-getting title and description that also includes your keywords.

YouTube has an analytics feature built into their product that allows you to see how many times your video was viewed and *where* it was viewed (on the YouTube website, embedded on your page, etc.).

Tips from the Trenches

Here are four additional suggestions for getting maximum use from YouTube:

1. Experiment! You won't know what kinds of videos will engage your potential audience until you try.
2. Don't try to be perfect or overly polished. You do not need a professional video producer to create content for your business. Don't put too much money into a single video; spread your bets across several different ones and learn as you go.
3. Don't invest too much in expensive equipment. Most current consumer digital cameras and microphones will do just fine. Even the camera on your smartphone is good enough for most purposes.
4. YouTube has a feature allowing you to add captions and clickable areas to your video. Use these to link your videos together.

Tracking Your Progress

With your Facebook fan page, track the number of fans you have and how that number is changing over time. Facebook has a feature called "insights" that lets you look at this data.

If you have a LinkedIn Group for your business, track how many members your Group has. Do a search for your industry keywords using the Group search feature to see how your Group ranks. This will give you a sense of how prominent your Group is within your industry.

For Twitter, track how your followers are growing, and what kind of engagement (retweets and favorites) you are getting. This measures your power and reach within Twitter by looking at your number of followers, the power of those followers, and the degree to which you're able to engage the Twitter community and get people to read and respond to your messages.

On YouTube, look at how many people are watching your channel. Do you get tens, hundreds, or thousands of views per video? Which types of video seem to be doing better than others?

Inbound in Action: FreshBooks

FreshBooks, the leader in cloud accounting software for small business owners, has a community of over 10 million people who use Fresh-Books to send, receive, print, and pay invoices. According to Mike McDerment, CEO of FreshBooks, although FreshBooks is technically a *software* company, it thinks of itself as a service company delivering *experiences*.

To remind the team of the company's focus and mission, Fresh-Books uses a concept known as 4E, which stands for "Execute on Extraordinary Experiences Everyday." It's this focus on delivering an experience that helps FreshBooks spread their brand online and has people talking about them. According to McDerment, customers are more likely to talk about their phenomenal *experience* with FreshBooks than they are about any specific capabilities of the software.

FreshBooks jumped into Twitter in January 2008, when they realized people were tweeting about the company and because they wanted to make it easier for their customers to communicate with them. The company now has over 20,000 followers and posts updates regularly (see Figure 7.6).

McDerment says, "While we answer questions and do support and hold contests on Twitter, we really just see Twitter as another way to deepen relationships with our customers. The truth is, while we collect dollars for the service that we offer, the currency of our business is relationships. Twitter, our blog, and our forums all help us share our culture with the world and learn more about our customers themselves. We like that."

McDerment further commented, "We started using Twitter because we saw that people were talking about us there. In fact, it freaked people out at first when they'd hear from us! We have a blog, we do a lot of e-mail and events, and we answer the phone. We just want to make it easy for people to communicate with us. Users choose the

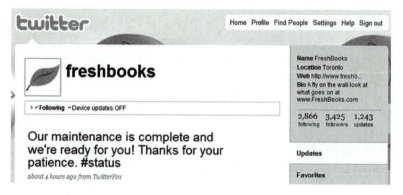

FIGURE 7.6   Screen Shot of a FreshBooks Update on Twitter

medium they like and we make it easy to connect. You know something really cool about our twittering? Now people are helping us do the support and question answering—it's amazing! So now what we are learning is to listen and let others do the talking."

One issue many businesses struggle with in social media is determining the right balance between personal and professional. When employees are representing the company online, what policies and guidelines should be in place? Do companies really have a say in what an employee might post to their Twitter accounts if the post is *not* related to the business? The FreshBooks approach to this problem is simple and refreshing. The company recognizes that they are hiring people into the company that often already have their own online networks developed (we discuss this later in the book when we talk about recruiting great people). FreshBooks encourages their employees to be themselves. "We don't want people to put on their work face," says McDerment, "we just want them to be themselves. So we try to stay out of the way of our team for the most part. Many of our customers are brought in through the personal relationships of our team members— people we meet at events, customers, friends, networks. Folks tend to use their personal profiles when participating where there are personal relationships."

That said, the company does have a separate business profile on Twitter (@freshbooks). This business Twitter account is managed by a small team within the company to ensure the tone is consistent. "We have some style guidelines like each post must be fun, playful, professional, and some obvious things like it should not include swearing." The company allows any employee to write articles for the blog, but does use blog "editors" who are responsible for ensuring the content is relevant for their audience.

Some words of advice from McDerment on how businesses that are just getting started with social media can build their reach online:

♦ Tell your story—that's what people respond to.
♦ Participate—follow up quickly to comments. Always remember you are setting the tone for your community.
♦ Be open and treat people as you would like to be treated. This builds trust, which is the foundation of any great relationship . . . and social media is all about building relationships.
♦ Listen—the greatest thing about communities is that they serve as a living, breathing focus group. If you listen right you can probably learn everything you need to know about your business.
♦ Finally—social media is a long road and a way of doing business; it's not a campaign. It needs long-term funding, support, and organizational commitment. The results will not be easy to tie to direct outcomes (read: sales), but the impact of a community that is well-nurtured grows exponentially.

To Do

♦ If you've somehow managed to resist signing up for Facebook, despite requests from your friends and family, go ahead and do it.
♦ Create a Facebook business page (also known as a fan page).
♦ Configure a subdomain that redirects to your Facebook page (example: http://facebook.yourcompany.com). This will make it easy for you to communicate the URL of your page until you eventually get a cleaner URL assigned to you by Facebook (i.e., facebook.com/yourcompany).
♦ The next time you host a business event (conference, webinar, training session, etc.), use Facebook events to invite people and get RSVPs.
♦ Look for your existing business contacts on Facebook. Invite them to connect with you.

- Make sure your LinkedIn profile is 100 percent complete. Link your profile to your business website and blog.
- Download and install the StumbleUpon toolbar.
- Create a LinkedIn user account and profile. If you already have one, make sure to update it so that it is current.
- Within the profile, add a link to your company's website. When you add this link, be sure to specify the anchor text (the text that users can click on) instead of accepting the default.
- Use the group search feature to find the biggest groups in your industry. Join these groups and start participating in the discussion.
- If you don't find a group that's focused on your industry, or the group is still small (< 500 members), create a new group.
- Make sure that you have reserved your company name as your Twitter username. Even though you may not elect to maintain separate Twitter accounts for yourself and your business, you should at least create an account for your business. It's free, it's easy, and you might need it later.
- Ensure that you complete your online profile including a brief bio, your location (city, state is sufficient), and a link to your website. Many people on Twitter are *looking* for interesting people to follow. Make sure they can find you.
- Use tools like Twitter Search to find influential Twitter users in your industry. Begin forging connections early.
- Create a StumbleUpon user account and download the toolbar.
- Select the categories that are the most relevant to your business.
- Start "stumbling" (click the Stumble button in the toolbar). Up-vote sites you like, down-vote those that you don't.
- When you come across interesting websites or articles, submit them to StumbleUpon (don't submit your own yet). Do this by clicking the "Thumbs Up" button in the toolbar when on the page.
- Begin befriending those who are submitting sites that you find highly relevant. Start building your friend list.

Chapter 8

Visual Content
A Picture Is Worth a Thousand Seconds

For the past few years, prominent speakers, bloggers, and authors have predicted a rise in "brand journalism." In other words, companies will increasingly employ professional journalists to report on both the organization's industry as well as broader topics that are likely to interest their buyers. And it turns out, they were right. From *Forbes* business reporter Tomas Kellner joining GE as a managing editor to the former editorial director of *Road Magazine* being named "brand journalist" at performance bicycle manufacturer Felt Bicycles, the trend is happening across companies of all sizes and in all industries.

Yet with each piece of marketing-produced content, the Internet becomes proportionally "noisier," and your buyer has incrementally less time to find your signal within all of the web's noise. This phenomenon has led to a rise in "visual communications," or design-heavy content that provides a degree of information disproportionate to the amount of time required to consume it. Infographics, animated "explainer" videos, interactive visualizations, and slide presentations that don't contain a single bullet have emerged to release some of the pressure on the customer's time. In response, we've seen a rise in specialty social networks that help people discover and share this visual content. Let's take a look at some of the most popular visual content communities.

SlideShare

SlideShare is a community built around the discovery and celebration of beautiful presentations. Initially dubbed "YouTube for PowerPoint," the company has since experimented with various forms of visual content, from videos to webinars to infographics—some more successfully than others. In 2012, LinkedIn acquired SlideShare to help increase content sharing on the professional social network. Today, SlideShare enjoys 215 million monthly page views.

Despite the diverse formats accepted by SlideShare, the community still tends to coalesce most around presentations. The company name itself has become an eponym, with marketers referring to creative presentations simply as "SlideShares."

It's not uncommon for a popular SlideShare to receive tens of thousands of views, particularly if the site features the presentation on its home page. Viral SlideShares can tally in the hundreds of thousands. We're proud of the fact that we produced the most popular business SlideShare of 2013 with over 1.2 million views. (You can see this deck at http://CultureCode.com.)

Because SlideShare's audience skews professional, the network also integrates with many marketing automation systems. If a marketer inserts a lead capture form into a presentation, SlideShare can import those leads into the organization's marketing database. This feature is particularly relevant for B2B marketers.

Visual.ly

Infographic design, a subset of the larger "data visualization" category, is a specialty within a specialty. Many connoisseurs of this content type frequent Visual.ly to procure, discover, or publish visual content, infographics in particular.

Visual.ly is both a marketplace that matches companies with data visualization professionals (to produce infographics, videos, interactive content, and presentations) as well as a "visual storytelling" community, where this type of content can be published, discovered, discussed, and shared. Content does not need to be produced by Visual.ly's design service in order to be shared in the community.

If you produce visual content, you may wish to share it in the Visual.ly community for a few reasons. Obviously, doing so will help active members discover your content, but more importantly, Visual.ly's authority will help your content rank well in Google, further increasing its reach. Visual.ly also provides embed code for content they host, which makes it easier for bloggers and journalists to share your content.

Pinterest

Pinterest has been a smash hit social network where people share, curate, and discover images and video by "pinning" them to a pinboard. Members pin images from their computer or images they've found on the Internet, sometimes by using a "Pin It" button installed in a browser. Pinterest launched to the public in 2010 and has an audience of 60 million monthly visitors in the United States, according to Com-Score, and 75 percent of them are using Pinterest via mobile devices. The audience is overwhelmingly female; by some accounts as many as 80 percent of members are women.

Pinterest has become a huge traffic driver—HubSpot, for example, gets more traffic from Pinterest than from Google+—and thus has become an appealing platform for marketers. Brands like Chobani, GE, and Peapod have avidly embraced Pinterest.

You should begin by adding a "Pin It" button to your website. That makes it easy for people to share things from your site on their pinboards. Each pin will include a link back the source. Those links are "no-follow links," meaning they don't boost your ranking on search engines like Google. But they will nevertheless draw people to your website and help you build your audience.

The key to doing well on Pinterest is to find incredibly great images. That's easier for some marketers than for others. Selling gorgeous luxury goods? You've got it made. But what if you're selling something like B2B software, which isn't exactly the stuff of which beautiful photos are made? It's a challenge, but it's not insurmountable.

Here are some things you can pin:

- Photos of your employees at a mixer or corporate event.
- Photos of your customers.
- Strong visuals that ran with your blog posts and ebooks.
- Infographics and data charts.
- A video gallery of your executives speaking at events.

Another tactic is to create a pinboard for your customers to use. Clothing retailer ModCloth created a Guest Pinner Gallery, where designers can pin examples of their work that they think ModCloth customers might like.

Some brands host contests. For example, you might ask customers to create pinboards with photos of themselves using your product or service and explaining why they love your brand. Best pinboard wins a prize.

Another tactic: you can tag pins with hashtags. So if you're running a campaign on Twitter and Google+ that uses a hashtag, you can put that same hashtag on related pins on Pinterest.

Finally, as with everything else you do, remember to measure. Use your analytics tools to determine which pins drive the most traffic, and see what works and what doesn't.

Instagram

Instagram is a massively popular photo-sharing and social networking service for mobile devices that lets people take photos, apply creative filters to them, and then share them on various social networks like Facebook and Twitter. Instagram also enables people to record and share short 15-second videos.

Instagram launched in 2010, and soon its rapid growth and popularity with a younger audience caught the attention of Facebook. In 2012, Facebook acquired Instagram for $1 billion, in part to establish a stronger presence on mobile devices. Instagram now claims to have 150 million monthly active users. Its demographic skews young. More than 90 percent of users are under the age of 35, and 68 percent are women, according to *Business Insider*.

Instagram accepts advertising, and these spots can be extremely effective. Ben & Jerry's reached 9.8 million people aged 18 to 35 in just eight days, according to *Business Insider*. But there are other ways for marketers to use Instagram. As with Pinterest, you can use Instagram as a way to widen the reach of a social media campaign, using visual content to amplify your message.

The original version of Instagram handled only still photos, but in June 2013 the service added support for video. That move was in part a response to Vine, the six-second video app that Twitter introduced in

January 2013 and which had started to steal the limelight from Instagram.

Brands like lululemon, Athletica, and Victoria's Secret were quick to pounce on Instagram's video feature. Fifteen seconds may not seem like much, but it's amazing what some creative folks have managed to do within these confines. Also keep in mind that if you've been working with Vine and its six-second limit, 15 seconds actually seems like a lot of time. Indeed, while Vines often look and feel like animated GIFs, with "InstaVids" some brands have been able to stretch a bit and create videos that have more of a narrative arc. Some videos feel like miniature TV commercials. You can use filters on Instagram video, just as you can with Instagram photos. Instagram has some editability features that Vine lacks.

Snapchat

Snapchat was created based on a deceptively simple idea: What if you had a photo-sharing app where pictures would vanish a few seconds after you opened them? At a time when people were obsessed with how much they were being tracked online, and concerned about the huge archives of photos and posts that we're all leaving around for eternity, the idea of a vanishing photo app was perhaps a stroke of genius.

You'd certainly think so based on the reception Snapchat received after it was launched in 2011. Snapchat won't say how many users it has, but it's been reported that the app has been downloaded 60 million times and that there are 30 million monthly active users. As of January 2014, Snapchat was drawing nearly 21 million monthly visitors in the United States alone, according to ComScore.

Snapchat even gave rise to a new category of social apps designed around content that is meant *not* to last. Suddenly, "ephemerality" was a hot new buzzword.

Snapchat lets you send images and video clips (up to 15 seconds long) to someone, and decide how long the content should remain visible—between 1 and 10 seconds.

The real appeal of Snapchat to marketers is the demographic profile of its audience. Snapchat's biggest adopters are 13 to 23 years old, and 70 percent of its users are female, according to AllThingsD.

Snapchat took some heat because it was seen as a "sexting tool" that teens could use to send naked pictures to each other, knowing the photos couldn't be shared or passed along. Some pundits believed that the presence of so much unsavory content would scare off advertisers. But apparently not, as brands have been testing the waters.

A frozen yogurt chain, 16 Handles, discovered that many of its customers were using Snapchat. The store sent out a promotion asking customers to take Snapchats of themselves eating 16 Handles yogurt and send the images to Love 16 Handles on Snapchat. Those who did received a coupon, which vanished in 10 seconds.

Taco Bell, known for its social media savvy, was among the first brands to embrace Snapchat, and used the service to announce the return of its "Beefy Crunch Burrito." Taco Bell started out by asking its Twitter followers to friend Taco Bell on Snapchat in order to receive a secret announcement. The next day, Taco Bell sent out a photo advertising the Beefy Crunch Burrito.

In October 2013, Snapchat expanded its service by introducing Snapchat Stories, a feature that stitches snaps together and forms a narrative. Snaps live for 24 hours before vanishing.

Vine

Can you really tell a story in a six-second video clip? You might be surprised by what people have managed do with Vine, the mobile app introduced by Twitter in 2013. Vine has given rise to a new roster of web celebrities, including "BatDad," the alter ego of Blake Wilson, a guy who became famous overnight after posting Vines of himself wearing a Batman mask in order to annoy and/or entertain his wife and kids.

There's even a Vine talent agency, Grape Story, run by social media consultant Gary Vaynerchuk. Vaynerchuk spotted Vine's potential as a marketing platform and was among the first to seize the opportunity. The company is doing "ridiculously well," Vaynerchuk said in 2013. "The engagement and awareness that we're driving for brands is ludicrous. This is like YouTube in 2008, or Twitter in 2007."

Vaynerchuk says the extremely limited nature of a Vine "forces people to pay attention. It's the same thing with Snapchat, where you know it's disappearing." And part of why Vines work is that the platform is still new, and the novelty itself is part of the appeal.

Vines have become a standard part of the social media arsenal at most big brands, including Toyota, Dove, Bacardi, Samsung, Lowe's, and Target. In September 2013, Dunkin' Donuts became the first brand to use Vine to create a television commercial—a five-second mini spot that aired on ESPN during the pre-game show for *Monday Night Football.*

Many marketers get overwhelmed or overly concerned with video production quality. But the quick upload, easy-to-use interface, and minimal emphasis on production quality is designed to encourage a little more experimentation. You can post "behind the scenes" videos of life at your office, quick product demos, or clips of a speaker to promote an upcoming webinar.

At HubSpot we used Vine to create a unique version of a regular event we call "Ask Me Anything," where our CMO, Mike Volpe, took questions via Twitter and then responded via six-second Vine clips rather than by typing answers in Twitter. We've found that Vine is a great way to develop a deeper, more personal connection with your audience, and to transform silent followers into serious brand evangelists.

Chapter **9**

Software and Tools as Content

I magine that you have a minimal marketing budget, zero content creators, and a goal of 100,000 unique monthly website visits. How is this even possible? For Takipi, a tool for web developers to identify bugs in their code, this was the challenge they faced. How they solved this common marketing conundrum is where this story gets exciting. They coded their way to 100,000 website visitors.

It all started by figuring out the assets they had at hand. In her blog post (www.startupmoon.com/coding-marketing-how-we-coded-our-way-to-100k-unique-visitors/), Iris Shoor, vice president of Product and Marketing at Takipi, says that the company has access to unique data from its customers. "The first time we published content that relied solely on developers' work was pretty random. When we had to choose in which Amazon region we wanted to store our data, we ran some tests and found out there was a big difference between the regions. Sounded like an interesting story. We spent an extra day improving our script and making sure we got the data right. The output was super interesting— the AWS Olympics. The results were featured on VentureBeat and published on our blog, bringing massive traffic of our target audience— over 15,000 unique visitors," Shoor wrote.

After hitting it big with data, Takipi moved to creating simple free tools to attract their target audience via inbound channels like search engines and social media. "We created java2014.org and scala2014.org. It's a simple calendar, with all Java and Scala events for this year. We outsourced collecting all the events, and used ODesk to build the events list. It's useful, has high SEO potential, and drives nice traffic of very targeted users," Shoor explained.

With these two examples, and other projects, Takipi was able to drive more than 100,000 unique website visitors by simply making their prospective customers' lives a little easier by writing code instead of prose.

Writing Code Instead of Text

The basis of inbound marketing is the same regardless of the delivery: provide value to build trust before engaging in a marketing or sales transaction. The delivery format, however, needs to differ depending on the strengths of your company. If your company employs web developers, free tools might be the right option for you. The challenge is that the time of a web developer is a very scarce resource. This means that as a marketer you have to make the right argument to win the time of the developer over other projects. Your executives want to put developer time where it will create the most enterprise value for the company.

As you would write an awesome outline for a blog post, you need to write a project plan. What if you have never built a free tool before? How do you know how to create a plan the executive team will support?

A great free tool starts with an important first step: Talk to real humans who you would want to use it. This may be simple advice, but many companies fail to do this. What are the common problems that your customers have? What are the issues that your salespeople get asked about over and over again?

From here you can begin to develop a project plan for your executives to approve and your web developer to use. These plans are like a creative brief that is often used in marketing to guide design projects. A strong project plan for a free tool should include:

◆ A clear definition of the target audience.
◆ A strong problem statement outlining the problem the tool will solve for the target audience.
◆ Core features needed in the initial version of the tool.
◆ A project timeline and milestones.

Having a project plan, even a simple one, will make communicating with your web developer and other stakeholders easier and will ensure that everyone on involved is aligned with the development of the tool.

Replace Humans with Machines

One of the first free tools we built in the early days of HubSpot was WebsiteGrader.com. Over the years, WebsiteGrader.com turned into MarketingGrader.com, which has now graded more than 4 million websites. It was a huge success for us. Marketing Grader is a great way to generate new inbound leads for our paid marketing software product because it had a strong viral coefficient. People would grade their own websites and then share their scores on Facebook, Twitter, LinkedIn, or e-mail and drive their connections to find out their own grades. We all love to be graded.

Not only did the tool spread across the web, it also had the added benefit of helping the user understand what aspects of his or her website and inbound marketing needed to be improved. This made an initial conversation with one of our salespeople a logical next step.

The kicker is that we didn't just magically come up with the idea for Website Grader. Instead, Brian was essentially doing this manually when he was demoing HubSpot software to prospective customers. Brian would compare them to their competition, and would show them problems with the search engine optimization of their websites. Dharmesh suggested that he could build a web application that automated everything Brian was doing manually each time he talked with a prospect. Like that, Website Grader was born!

Another approach is to build a free tool on an existing platform with its own audience. This is the approach that InsightSquared, a software company that provides simple business intelligence software to Salesforce users, took. According to Zorian Rotenberg, VP of Marketing and Sales at InsightSquared, "We came up with our free apps by finding a single, tangible need that applied broadly across our target market. But it also had to be a need that we could address with a relatively simple concept that tied back (at least loosely) to our overall offering. We spend a ton of time helping and working with new and experienced sales and marketing teams, so we know the pain points they face day-to-day. We've built a number a free tools to deliver better analytics and insights to Salesforce users."

The InsightSquared team built several free tools for Salesforce users including: Sales Funnel, an app that instantly calculates the stage-by-stage conversion rates for your opportunity stages and presents it in an intuitive, CEO-friendly funnel report, and Sales Leaderboard, a tool that enables executives to motivate their teams through healthy competition and by celebrating reps' successes.

How have these tools performed for InsightSquared? According to Rotenberg, "Our free apps generate some of our best performing leads. By allowing leads to experience the strength of our product firsthand, we create a very receptive audience for our inside sales team. Our conversion rate from free app leads is almost 20 times that of our average campaign."

Take a look around your business. What is something that one or more of your employees do repeatedly to demonstrate value to prospective customers? Automating this action, if possible, is an awesome place to start for your first free marketing tool.

Provide a Next Step

It is key to remember that your free tool is part of your marketing funnel. Most often it will be a way to attract more attention at the top of your marketing funnel. Because the use of your free tool is likely the first interaction a person is having with your company it is critical that your tool includes a next step to move him or her through the marketing funnel. When building Website Grader we created a feature that allowed the person to get an e-mail version of his or her report and opt in to additional marketing e-mails from HubSpot.

E-mail opt-in is only one way that you can provide the next step in your marketing funnel. Additionally, you can also include calls-to-action to other lead generation conversion events on your website, and have users connect with your company on social media channels or any other way that brings them closer to being a long-term member of your marketing audience.

Kill Bad Tools Quickly

You don't have a crystal ball. You don't know if a free tool will catch fire or fizzle a few days after launch. While you need to solve for your prospect and build a tool that is simple to use, you ultimately don't have control over how successful the tool is going to be long-term. However, you can control how long you support a tool that isn't effectively helping you accomplish your marketing goals.

If a tool isn't working, shut it down. Don't spend precious marketing and development resources on a project that isn't working. It is easy to feel that you have to "make it work" because you put a lot of time and effort into building the tool. Resist this feeling. Admit it didn't work and move on to the next free tool idea or marketing campaign. The key to inbound marketing is to iterate and improve. Sometimes this means getting rid of projects that aren't delivering to make way for new projects that have great potential.

Tools Don't Market Themselves

Products don't market themselves. This is a great urban myth spread by companies that overinvest in product development at the expense of marketing resources. When you decide to build a free tool as part of your inbound marketing mix, you also need to create a promotional campaign to support the launch of the tool to the public.

You might think it's best to start out by limiting your tool to a small group of beta users. Companies do this because they believe they can build a sense of exclusivity by only letting a small number of people use the tool. They expect those beta users will begin to discuss the tool online, and that this will create demand from other people. With free tools, however, this approach is not effective.

A more effective approach is often to preview the free tool to influencers and the media. A few days prior to launching the tool, give industry influencers and reporters exclusive access so that they can write articles and blog posts that can be released the day you launch the tool. You can also get quotes from the industry influencers and use them in your launch materials.

In addition to the prelaunch preview you also need to build a coordinated inbound marketing campaign. This campaign should include the following marketing aspects:

- Blog posts to promote the tool.
- Feature promoting the tool on your website home page.

- E-mail marketing campaign to existing contacts.
- Scheduled social media messages promoting the launch of the tool.
- Online advertising to support the launch (Twitter, Facebook, LinkedIn, etc.).

Don't overlook the power of an effective inbound marketing campaign. It can't fix a bad tool, but it can supercharge the growth of a good one.

Inbound in Action: Wealthfront

Wealthfront is the world's largest and fastest-growing automated investment service. Wealthfront believes that everyone deserves sophisticated investment advice. Much of their inbound marketing strategy is built on creating content and resources for their audiences that support this mission. For example, Wealthfront publishes several articles weekly to its Knowledge Center that serve to provide readers with actionable financial strategies and guidance, provided by expert authors, that are accessible to nonclient and client readers alike.

Additionally, Wealthfront has built a series of free tools that readers can use to simulate data, providing important insights into trends and historical performance that is useful to financial decision-making.

One such tool, Wealthfront's Post-IPO Stock Sale Simulator, models stock data from 10 different tech companies together with financial performance results of the company stock treated with five different sales strategies. Because it is impossible to time the market, it can be difficult to strategize how to buy and sell stocks, and what effect an individual's selling decisions would have on her portfolio. Wealthfront's IPO Stock Sale Simulator is an evergreen tool that enables users to evaluate the performance of a portfolio as a result of making a variety of selling/holding decisions.

Creating a tool with high utility prolongs its lifespan, and for Wealthfront, the Stock Sale Simulator is among the top content items users return to and share with friends, over a year after its release. Additionally, since the topic of post-IPO sales planning comes up with every new IPO announcement in Silicon Valley and beyond, the content and data presented in the Stock Sale Simulator is newly relevant each time a tech company announces this major milestone.

Another such tool that Wealthfront created to provide a high value data source for its readers is the Startup Salary and Equity Compensation Tool. Since the majority of Wealthfront clients are millennials with jobs in the tech industry, many will change jobs or careers several times before they retire. Each time, they will be pondering the worth of their compensation offers, sizing up the total packages and wondering if they are commensurate with their expectations of their own market values. Wealthfront collected data from hundreds of private companies, spanning over 14,000 nonexecutive salaries and modeled a tool for users to be able to assess their compensation offers relative to industry, size of company, stage of growth, and the level of their position.

Like the Stock Sale Simulator Tool, this asset continues to be among the most highly trafficked sources of content that Wealthfront has released for public consumption.

To Do

1. Interview your customers to get ideas for free tools.
2. Look at any successful free tools in your industry and analyze why that tool is successful.
3. Outline and build your marketing campaign in parallel with the development of the tool.
4. _____
5. _____
6. _____

Part III

Converting Customers

The purpose of business is to create and keep a customer.

—Peter F. Drucker

Chapter 10

Convert Visitors into Leads

You now know how to get your website and other content found by your target market using various methods, including how to pull people into your business using blogs, Google, and social media. However, simply getting visitors to your website isn't enough. You need to *convert* these visitors into qualified leads and eventually paying customers. The true power of inbound marketing lies in its ability to not only stretch the top of your sales funnel (and pull more people in), but also stretch the middle (get more to convert).

Conversion is the art and science of encouraging site visitors to further engage with your business. You do this by helping people take some sort of action: subscribing to your e-mail newsletter, filling out a form, or requesting a demo. It's important to provide a variety of different ways for visitors to further engage—versus simply calling your company or buying something from your site. This is because not everyone who visits your site is at the same place in the buying or sales cycle—meaning some people are ready to buy now and some may not be ready until three to six months from now or longer. It's better to provide people with options to engage at whatever level they're comfortable, from handing over only a name and e-mail address for your e-newsletter to filling out a longer form for a white paper, webinar, or demo. (We cover how to nurture those leads who aren't yet ready to do business in Chapter 12.)

It's also important to understand that site visitors do not always enter your site from the home page, which is another reason why you shouldn't think of your website as a "brochure." More often than not, when someone finds your website via a referral from Google or another third-party site, they'll be taken to the web page that most closely matches what they were looking for. This could be a page with information about your product, a blog article, or any other web page on your site. As a result, when thinking about conversions, think about the potential action a site visitor can take to further engage with you when he or she lands on *any* page within your website.

Once you get that visitor on your page, you need to show him or her exactly the action to take—and you do this with a *compelling* call-to-action. We can't stress enough the importance of a call-to-action. The difference between a weak call-to-action (e.g., a Contact Us page with an e-mail address on it) and a compelling one can mean the difference between a half a percent visitor-to-lead conversion rate and a 5 percent visitor-to-lead conversion rate. On a site with 1,000 visitors per day, that is the difference between 5 qualified leads per day and 50 qualified leads per day. Next, we describe the four qualities of a killer call-to-action: valuable, easy to use, prominent, and action oriented (VEPA—see Figure 10.1).

Compelling Calls-to-Action

Site visitors were attracted to your site due to your *remark*able content; it will require an equally compelling call-to-action to convert them into qualified leads. The visitors you are drawing in are asking themselves the following questions:

"Why should I click this button and give them my information?"

"What's in it for me?"

"Is the value of the thing I am getting worth giving up my e-mail address for?"

People have become quite skeptical about giving out their contact information, so there needs to be an obvious perception of value that exceeds their expectations and overcomes this skepticism. Generally, businesses underestimate how valuable offers need to be in order to obtain people's contact information, so it's a good practice to think about a whole series of increasingly valuable offers and experiment with them. You'll remember our adage from earlier in the book, "You've gotta give to get!"

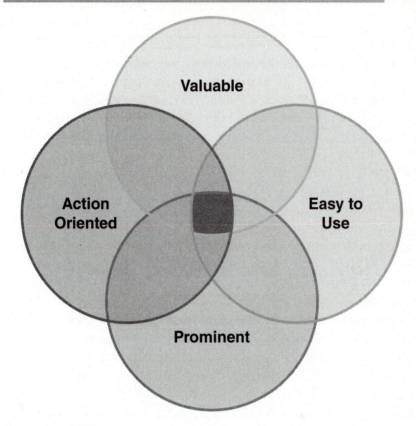

FIGURE 10.1 VEPA

Good calls-to-action typically involve giving your users helpful information, to enable them to do their jobs better or help them become more valuable to a future employer. The giveaway or offer is generally more *remark*able content, including:

♦ Webinars
♦ White papers or reports
♦ An ebook
♦ A 30-minute expert consultation
♦ Research studies
♦ A free class, demo, or trial offer

Experiment with various types of offers to see which generate the best conversion rates.

EASY TO USE

Web usability expert Steve Krug wrote a great book about web design titled *Don't Make Me Think*. His basic premise is that when people arrive at your site, they shouldn't have to think about what to do next. The title of his book sums up how you should consider your calls-to-action: They should be clear and simple (few words) and should indicate what action to take and the result of that action.

PROMINENT

To encourage conversion, your offer needs to stand out—it should pop! What can you do to ensure that your offers are prominent?

Placement on the page is critical. The call-to-action should sit near the top of the page so that the visitor can see it without having to scroll down the page.

The call-to-action should also be a clickable image with a relatively large font—versus a text link buried amid page clutter—with white space around it so that the eye is drawn naturally to it. It should also be highlighted with color to make it stand out. (See Figure 10.2.)

Every page on your site should have a call-to-action, not just your home page and landing pages, and the calls-to-action should be context sensitive. For example, your product page might have a "see a demonstration" call-to-action while your services page might have a "get a free 30-minute consultation" call-to- action.

ACTION ORIENTED

Your call-to-action should begin with a verb and tell the visitor what action to take. Here are some of the action-oriented calls-to-action we have seen work well:

- ◆ Test Yourself Against Your Peers
- ◆ Get Your Grade
- ◆ Win Our Contest

FIGURE 10.2   Screen Shot of a Call-to-Action

Mistakes to Avoid

One of the lowest converting calls-to-action is "Contact Us." If your site uses this call-to-action, make it a priority to change it as soon as possible.

A related mistake is using an e-mail address to have people contact you versus filling out a form. Using an e-mail address is problematic for three reasons. First, you want to capture your users' contact information in a database in order to nurture these leads should they not be ready to buy just yet; capturing them manually is difficult to do when you're only getting e-mails from them. Second, you invite spammers who scrape e-mail addresses from websites. And third, people without desktop e-mail applications, such as Outlook, often cannot open those e-mail links. Every contact e-mail address on your site should be replaced with a short web form. Remember, the goal is to make it as easy as possible for the user. We talk more about forms in the next chapter.

Optimizing Through Experimentation

In order to maximize your prospect-to-lead-conversion percentage, it is important that you test multiple calls-to-action with different VEPA (valuable, easy to use, prominent, and action oriented) emphasis. Testing one variable, such as the offer or the headline of a page, is called an A/B split test and is relatively easy to conduct. You test your "control" offer or headline against another—with all other variables (colors, fonts, page layout, etc.) remaining the same. Testing two or more variables at the same time is called "multivariate testing." As you test small changes, you'll be surprised at the differences in conversion rates. You can do endless experiments, but you should focus on those with increasingly valuable calls-to-action and increasingly prominent calls-to-action.

In order to do those tests, we recommend you have your site set up so that you (not your IT guy) can make changes and run tests on your calls-to-action very easily.

Tracking Your Progress

It's important that you track the percentage of visitors who convert into qualified leads over time. As you make changes to your calls-to-action and you improve VEPA, you will see changes in your conversion rates. Obviously, higher is better with this metric!

As a rule of thumb, you should have at least a 1 percent visitor-to-conversion rate on untargeted traffic. Having a conversion rate of over 5 percent is quite good on untargeted traffic.

Inbound in Action: Google

Google is a master at making/testing changes on their site to increase conversion rates. Before becoming CEO of Yahoo!, Marissa Mayer was an executive at Google. She told a story about how the Google team debated which shade of blue would convert best on one of their properties. The answer was not obvious, so they tested 40 different shades of blue to see which one converted the most visitors into committed users.

Now, you don't have as much traffic as Google, so it would take too long to get enough data to make a test with 40 different variations. Having said that, you should continually question core assumptions about your site by running a few different variations of calls-to-action, landing page design, and form length to find the optimal conversion rates.

To Do

1. Ensure your site has a call-to-action on every page and is set up such that *you* can change these calls-to-action and measure the changes in conversion rates from visitor to lead.

2. Make sure your calls-to-action are valuable, easy to use, prominent, and action oriented (VEPA).

3. Measure your overall visitor-to-lead conversion rate on your site religiously and work to increase it through testing.

4. _____

5. _____

6. _____

Chapter 11

Convert Prospects into Leads

The previous chapter talked about calls-to-action that convert untargeted traffic. This chapter talks about how to use specialized web pages (landing pages) to convert high percentages of more targeted traffic that is driven through programs, such as e-mail marketing or pay-per-click (PPC) campaigns.

You can use landing pages to channel recipients of your individual outreach programs. For example, if your e-mail newsletter has a link in it about biotech patent law, it is much better to have the link go to a page built solely around biotech patent law with an offer and form on it, rather than your home page or a generic page about patent law that touches on industries other than biotech. The same holds true for corresponding with your list through Twitter, LinkedIn Groups, and SMS (text) updates, among others. (It is time we all started thinking beyond e-mail as the only vehicle for communicating with our marketing database.)

You can also use landing pages to build specific content for search traffic, specifically pay per click or Google AdWords. If you want to get more value out of the money you're spending on AdWords, then you should send AdWords traffic to a specific landing page on the topic of the ad you are buying rather than sending them to your generic home page. You can increase conversion rates and return on investment (ROI) by several times by making PPC landing pages extremely relevant.

Landing Page Best Practices

The landing page is the final step in converting a visitor to a lead. It's where the visitor ultimately decides whether to proceed with the

Click to LOOK INSIDE!

**The Innovator's Dilemma: V
(Management of Innovation**
by <u>Clayton M. Christensen</u> (Author) "Whe
sage advice..." (<u>more</u>)
Key Phrases: <u>value network framework</u>, <u>per</u>
<u>Trend Report</u> (<u>more...</u>)
★★★★☆ ☑ (<u>166 customer reviews</u>)
- -
List Price: $35.00

FIGURE 11.1   Screen Shot of Amazon.com's Page for Clayton Christensen's Book

transaction of trading his or her contact information for the information being offered. A good landing page can convert 50 percent of its visitors into qualified leads while a poor one will convert less than 1 percent. Using landing page best practices can dramatically improve your conversion rates and lower your cost per lead. Some best practices for landing pages are described next.

MATCHING

It's important that you match the content on your landing page with the content on your call-to-action as precisely as possible. Amazon's landing pages are great examples on how to do this. If you search Google for "Clayton Christensen book," Amazon's Google listing brings you to the following page with Christensen's best-selling book on it (see Figure 11.1).

BUILDING TRUST

In order to increase ROI, your landing page should project a professional image, including professional design, well-written copy, and other factors. A poorly designed page or dubious product claims may raise concerns in your visitor's mind about providing information to your company. Your landing page should efficiently and quickly convey value and show that your company is reputable and trustworthy. Figure 11.2 is an example of a page that might not convey the level of trust required to convert a visitor into a lead.

GO NAKED

Your landing page has one function only: to get people to fill out your form! Landing page best practices indicate that reducing the number of

FIGURE **11.2** Untrustworthy Landing Page

offers on the page and removing potentially distracting navigation to other sections of your website will increase ROI. Why is that? Because removing all this extraneous "stuff" gives people no other option except to fill out the form (see Figure 11.3). You have spent money and effort in order to convince a visitor to land on the most targeted page you have, relative to what that person is interested in, so don't give them an opportunity (or worse, enticement) to leave the landing page and go somewhere less targeted on your site.

GRAPHICS MATTER

Including lots of images on a standard web page can work against you because images don't help improve your Google rankings (remember, the search engine spider can't "read" images). In the case of landing pages, SEO isn't your main priority, so this is one place where eye-popping graphics can really work. (See Figure 11.4.) Just make sure you don't overdo it so that it becomes a distraction from the main goal. You need to *test* your landing pages to figure out what maximizes conversions.

KEEP IT SIMPLE

You've drawn a visitor to a page where the single option available is to provide you with the information you need to convert him or her to a

FIGURE 11.3   Screen Shot of Landing Page without Navigation

FIGURE 11.4   Screen Shot of Landing Page with Eye-Popping Graphics

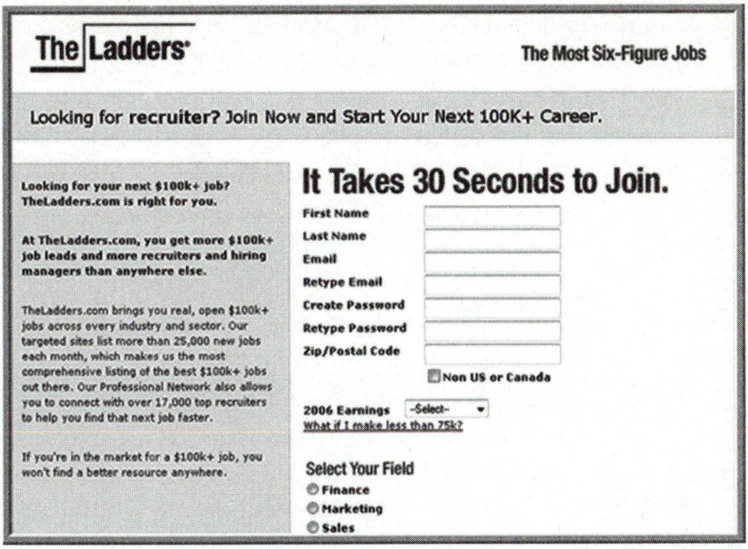

FIGURE 11.5 Screen Shot of Simple Landing Page

lead. (See Figure 11.5.) Now is not the time to bombard this person with more options or additional information to read. If you decide that you need any explanatory text, keep it very short; a bulleted list is a good model.

In order to maximize your prospect-to-lead conversion percentage, it's important that you *test* multiple landing page designs with different language, content length, images, and so on. As with testing calls-to-action that we discussed in Chapter 10, you'll be surprised at the conversion rate differences between small changes in your landing pages. In order to do those tests, we recommend you have your site set up so that you (not your IT person) can easily make changes and run tests on your landing pages with conversion rate metrics. Using the best practices we've outlined here and experimenting with them can dramatically improve your visitor-to-lead conversion rates on your forms.

Creating Functional Forms

Once your visitors have clicked through from an e-mail, pay-per-click ad, or e-newsletter, you want them to come to a landing page with a form on it, versus a landing page with a link to an e-mail address on it.

If you give them a link to an e-mail address, they might send you an e-mail, but you'll then have to remember to manually add this name to your database. Instead, use software that will permanently capture lead information for use down the road. Every person who fills out a call-to-action on your site should be permanently captured and nurtured.

Short

Although it's tempting to ask your prospect a lot of questions, visitors are much more likely to ignore long forms or to abandon them before completing the process. Keep your forms simple and short by asking only the most important questions, such as name and e-mail address, and if the person is in the market for your product or services. (This will help you weed out those people who are downloading your information for other reasons, such as writing blog posts, trade publication articles, or white papers, or because they are your competition!) Your sales organization will want you to ask for more information, but you need to be very careful to balance the number of questions with conversion ratios. We recommend you keep the form short and then gather more information (e.g., addresses) as you move along in the sales process.

Above the Fold

Keep at least part of the form visible to readers above the fold so that they don't have to scroll down the page.

Not Sensitive

If you ask for sensitive information, such as a Social Security numbers or company revenues, you'll dramatically lower your conversion rates. Keep the information you ask for relatively benign and collect more sensitive information later in the sales process.

Simple

Do not ask your prospects questions that require them to go elsewhere to find the information. Nor should you ask questions that require prospects to "think." Thinking and research equals lower conversion rates. In the same vein, don't provide "cancel" or "clear" buttons, as they confuse visitors and often lead to mistakenly clearing the forms, which

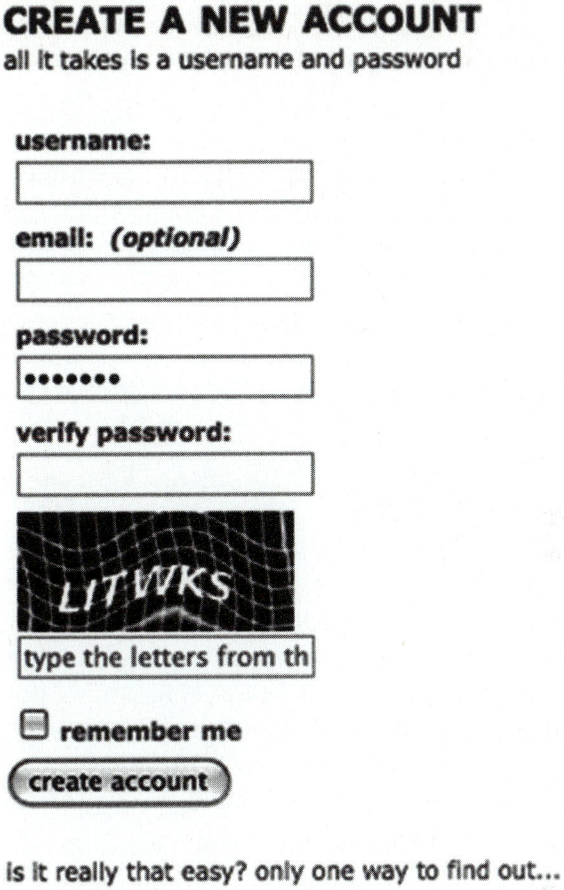

CREATE A NEW ACCOUNT
all it takes is a username and password

username:

[   ]

email: *(optional)*

[   ]

password:

[•••••••   ]

verify password:

[   ]

[type the letters from th]

☐ remember me

(create account)

is it really that easy? only one way to find out...

FIGURE 11.6 Screen Shot of a Simple, Functional Form

irritates users and forces them to re-enter the data, often resulting in them just giving up. (See Figure 11.6.)

TRUST

One of the challenges with getting people to fill out forms is addressing their concerns about how their data will be used. For example, if you ask for someone's e-mail address, the visitor might wonder whether you'll rent or sell their information to third parties (a common practice in some industries). To increase your credibility and trust, it's useful to have a clear privacy policy explaining what you will and will not do with people's information. You can link to your privacy policy right from your form. Having this kind of transparency increases the likelihood that users will complete your form.

Auto Responder

Make sure you configure your form so that prospects receive an e-mail confirmation when it is filled out, with a further call-to-action, in order to continue to pull them into your funnel to extract more information about them.

As mentioned before, in order to do those tests, we recommend you have your site set up so that you (not your IT person) can easily make changes and run tests on your forms and conversion rates.

Going Beyond the Form

The good thing about the web today is that you know a lot more about the people who fill out your form than what is in the form. Configure your site so that you can track every page prospect's visit, every comment they make on your blog, and the company for whom they work. (This is a little spooky, but worth doing.) All of this information should go into your database, along with the form information; having this comprehensive view of your prospect on hand when you follow up will increase your likelihood of closure. For example, someone who went to two pages on your site and filled out a form with their Gmail address should be treated much differently than someone who visited your site five times, made two supportive comments on your blog, visited the same pharmaceutical case study on your site three times, and is coming from Pfizer's office building.

A Word of Caution

Many marketers in mid-size and large companies spend 80 percent of their time worrying about conversion rates and 20 percent of their time on getting more visitors in the first place. The biggest problem most companies face is not converting more visitors to leads, but rather getting more visitors in the first place. For most businesses, it is prudent to flip those ratios around so that you are spending 80 percent of your time getting more visitors, and 20 percent of your time getting higher conversion rates.

PAGE NAME	PAGE VIEWS	SUBMISSIONS	CONVERSION RATE
5 Tips - 10 tip 5	629	2	.32%
5 Tips - 11 resources	507	15	2.96%
5 Tips - 2	3410	172	5.04%
5 Tips - 3 outbound inbound	4073	54	1.33%

FIGURE 11.7 Landing Page Metrics

Tracking Your Progress

You need to track a few metrics regarding every landing page, such as visitors, conversions, and resulting conversion rate. Measuring these with different variations of the landing page layout, as described earlier can help you optimize your landing page for maximum results. You want to think about landing pages as continuous improvement machines that constantly get better with testing and tweaking. As a rule of thumb, you should be getting at least 15 percent of the people who come to a landing page to convert and fill out the form. If you are getting over 50 percent, you are doing an exceptional job. (See Figure 11.7.)

Inbound in Action: Zappos

An online shoe retailer and an inbound marketing success story, Zappos has grown to over $1 billion in revenue since its beginning 10 years ago. Although most people buy shoes from the shoe store in their local malls, a store can carry only so much inventory due to space limitations, which in turn limits selection. Because Zappos is online, they have an almost unlimited inventory. Where this really works well is when you have feet with slightly strange dimensions—really wide or really big. Most mall-based shoe stores won't bother carrying inventory for size 18 sandals, for example, because the market for them is so limited. For people who wear size 18, Zappos is one of the few places to shop.

Zappos spent considerable time building a web presence and ensuring their site was well optimized. "Google has a really sophisticated crawler," says Matt Burchard, director of Content and Direct Online Marketing, "and is able to identify the exact pages for specific products, such as size 18 shoes." Zappos also spends considerable time monitoring and analyzing its search data. If the company notices that customers are searching for something specific for which the company doesn't have a landing page, they will manually build one.

When you search Google for size 18 shoes, and you click the Zappos listing in the organic search results (Zappos uses both paid and organic search practices to generate inbound leads), you come to a landing page that features only size 18 shoes. Zappos includes controls on the page to configure for size and width (up to EEEEEEEE by the way!), but the control to get the user to other sizes is just set on 18. Zappos is smart—when they get someone interested in size 18 shoes, they do not send them to a page that makes them navigate down to find the size 18 shoes.

Incidentally, Zappos is also a master at leveraging social media and blogs to get found by customers. Many of their employees are active Twitter users and the company writes a number of blogs as well.

To Do

1. Ensure your website is configured so that *you* can set up a landing page, change it, and measure the impact on conversion rate without help from IT people.
2. Ensure your website is configured so that you can set up forms, change them, and measure the impact on conversion rate without help from IT people.
3. Make sure your landing pages match your call-to-action, build trust, are naked, have graphics, and are simple to use.
4. Make sure your forms are short, above the fold, not asking for sensitive information, are simple, build trust, and have autorespond.
5. _____
6. _____
7. _____

Chapter 12

Convert Leads to Customers

Once you have a steady flow of leads coming in due to your inbound marketing efforts, you can then start to convert these leads into paying customers.

Grading and Scoring Your Leads

Not all inbound leads are created equal. They don't all close at a higher rate, faster, or with less effort than outbound leads. Depending on your business and your product/service, some inbound leads can close in as little as 15 minutes while others can take three to six months or more (this is especially true for B2B, where the sales cycle is much longer). It's important, then, to measure not just the quantity of leads, but the *quality* of your inbound leads in order to determine the effectiveness of your marketing and to allocate your time following up on your best leads. By quality we mean those leads that are likely to become good customers. You can be getting hundreds of leads every month but if these leads don't convert over time, you're either not creating the right kind of *remark*able content targeted to your audience or you have offers that bring in lots of untargeted traffic that happens to convert.

MEANWHILE, 320 MILES TO THE SOUTHEAST...

To measure the quality of leads, you'll need to somehow *grade* them, with the higher value leads getting a better grade. You can use specialized software applications to automatically calculate the lead grade for you or you can manually grade leads yourself. Either way, the lead grade should be stored in your database along with the other information about your leads.

How should the inbound lead grade be calculated? There's no one answer to this. It depends on your business and how sophisticated a formula you want to use. The following are some of the factors that can go into the calculation of the lead grade.

REFERRAL CHANNEL

How did the lead find you? Did the person come via a Google search, a link from a blog, a social media site, or a link from your e-mail newsletter? The referral sources that have converted best in the past should influence this weighting. This means you'll need to either begin keeping track of your referral sources or go back and analyze your data if you do track this information. We recommend you analyze the previous two years of referral lead sources to see which generate the best leads for you.

WEBSITE VISITS

Did the lead just visit your website once, or did they visit it many times? Did they visit recently or was it months ago? Did they look at specific web pages indicating that they're further along in the buying process? For example, someone who looked at your pricing page is likely to be a better lead than someone who looked at the management team bios.

CALLS-TO-ACTION TAKEN

Usually, a visitor becomes a lead by completing some call-to-action (such as completing a lead form). As we discuss in Chapter 6, you should have several types of calls-to-action on your site, with different forms, such as request a demo, download a white paper, request a call with a sales representative, and so on, because some lead forms generate higher value leads than others. Also, leads that completed more than one call-to-action are likely better qualified. If a lead downloaded a white paper, registered for a webinar, *and* requested a demo, that's likely a better lead than someone who had requested only one of those things.

FORM RESPONSES

On your lead forms, you often ask a series of questions. Examples include: Are you a small business or large enterprise? What industry are you in (financial services, healthcare, manufacturing)? Do you sell to consumers or businesses? Whatever the questions are, each tells you information about the lead. It's highly likely that certain types of leads (those that responded to questions in a certain way) are more qualified than others. If you're selling legal services primarily to large Fortune 500 companies with lots of different brands, someone who tells you that they're a small business is likely not a high-value lead. It is tempting to ask many questions on your lead forms simply to get better data on the leads, so that they can be graded more accurately. As discussed earlier, this is often a mistake. You should ask for the minimal amount of data that is *just enough* to make a reasonable quality assessment. Ask too many questions, and the web visitor won't become a lead in the first place and an opportunity is lost.

All of these factors can be combined into a predictive formula that calculates the lead grade based on the available data. You generally preconfigure this formula into your lead management software, assign specific points to various factors, and calculate a final grade based on those points. Another powerful approach is to use closed-loop grading. This refers to the ability to automatically infer the lead-grading formula by looking at the data of leads coming in historically.

Nurturing Your Leads

Based on the grade, some leads are qualified and ready to be handed to sales for follow-up. Other leads may not yet be ready to buy. Many businesses make the mistake of ignoring these leads or handing them to a sales rep who disqualifies them because they are not ready to buy this quarter. Because salespeople work on commission, their tendency is to pluck the "low hanging fruit" first—which is why they concentrate on closing sales with qualified leads and ignoring all others. This is unfortunate since there's a lot of value in these leads—because many of them will *eventually* buy. Therefore, if you don't stay in front of these leads on a consistent basis, there's a good chance these people will buy from a competitor who has been keeping in touch. The unqualified leads that weren't sent to a sales rep or disqualified should be placed into a lead nurturing program until they take further action that increases their grade enough to be handed (back) to a sales rep.

The idea behind lead nurturing is to maintain ongoing communication and dialog with these leads so that when they're ready to buy, your product is at the top of their minds. Nurturing leads often occurs only through e-mail, but it should include a variety of channels, as appropriate to your business, including phone calls. How often you stay in touch should be based on the length of your sales cycle. For example, if you're a B2B company with a complex sales cycle that extends over many months, you should probably limit yourself to one to two messages a month.

The nurturing program should involve different segments of leads. For example, the leads that came through your "download a white paper call to action" will get one set of messages while the leads that came through your industry trade show will get another. Just as you want your landing pages to be specific to your call-to-action, you want your nurturing messages to be specific to the call-to-action, as well.

The information that you send through your lead nurturing program should be *useful* and always include a compelling call-to-action. Similar to the blog content we described earlier, the content in your nurturing program shouldn't sell too hard. Leads in your nurturing program should *want* to hear from you because in each interaction with the lead, you should be creating value. A great example of *remark*able content sent to us through a lead nurturing campaign comes from Venator Partners, one of many executive search firms in our area. We receive their nurturing e-mails weekly and are drawn in by a few of their *remark*able features. For example, the e-mails always have a new inspirational quote, such as this one from Ralph Waldo Emerson: "Our greatest glory consists not in never falling . . . but in rising every time we fall." The messages provide a comprehensive list of the previous week's IPO filings, venture fundings, and executive moves—incredibly useful information that's packed into one place. Included with this useful information is a graph plotting these three things over time (see Figure 12.1). Because their nurturing campaign is remarkable enough for us to look at each week, when we're ready to hire an executive search firm, Venator Partners will be one of the firms on our short list.

We have a word of caution about spending lots of time or money on lead grading and nurturing. The problem most companies have is getting more leads, not sorting through the leads they have by grading and nurturing them. Before you spend days and weeks setting up fancy grading and nurturing systems, it is advisable to get your lead creation machine cranking first.

Broadening Your Reach

By doing the things we have been talking about so far in this book, you'll begin broadening your *reach*, a term that we use to describe

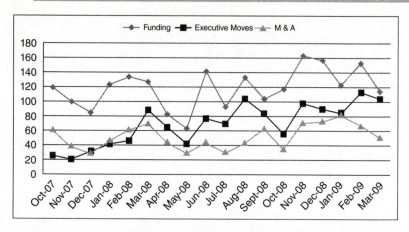

FIGURE 12.1   From Venator Partners Weekly E-Mail

the total number of marketing contacts you have. Traditionally, marketers think about their contact database as their e-mail and/ or direct mail list, but with inbound marketing you should expand your definition to include all of the people you can reach through e-mail, blog subscriptions, Twitter, Facebook, LinkedIn, and other social networks.

When you want to influence your marketplace about something important, such as a new service offering, your reach should go beyond your e-mail list and expand to all of your followers. The major benefit of communicating with your market through channels like social media and blogs, rather than e-mail, is that your market is pre-programmed to ignore everything coming through e-mail as propaganda while relying on their colleagues and social media sites for new information. Your e-mail audience is unlikely to physically *respond* to an e-mail blast (especially when the e-mail address the message is coming from is noreply@yourcompany.com), but they are much more likely to engage by commenting back to you when they are notified about new offerings through social media contacts and your blog. Also, notices of new offerings sent through social media sites are much more likely to go viral. For example, if you announce your new service offering on Twitter and one of your followers tweets back, then their followers' attention will be drawn to your announcement. The same holds true for Facebook, LinkedIn, and your blog.

Tracking Your Progress

You can measure several things in the lead-to-customer conversion stage addressed in this chapter, but the most important one is how efficiently you are closing customers with your marketing efforts.

You can tweak your landing pages and conversion forms by measuring the conversion rate on your landing pages, to determine if you're leaking too many visitors and thus lowering your conversion rate. Often, creating more targeted content and simplifying the form can improve your conversion rate dramatically.

Finally, you should track the effectiveness of your lead-nurturing programs. For example, when you send an e-mail out to your list, how many of your subscribers actually click through on one of the links in the message? If you're selling a product, how many purchase it? Measuring how well your lead-nurturing programs are performing will help you get a better sense of the *value* of a lead, even when that lead is not yet ready to buy.

Inbound in Action: Kiva

Not-for-profit Kiva's mission is to connect people through lending for the sake of alleviating poverty. The organization's person-to-person micro-lending website empowers individuals to lend directly to unique entrepreneurs around the globe.

Kiva has built an exceptional level of reach in a relatively short period of time using inbound marketing. The kiva.org website is currently one of the top 10,000 websites in terms of traffic, according to Alexa, and has over 212,000 members in its Facebook group. By any measure, this is an online success story. But, what's particularly impressive is that they have done this with a relatively low budget (remember, inbound marketing is not about the "width of your wallet").

Most non-profit websites simply state the organization's mission, and share some brochureware information (in many cases, the content is actually the *same* as the printed brochure!). Kiva goes well beyond that in getting their existing community to help extend their message.

One example is the "Email Your Friends" feature on the website. Kiva provides sample text that users can simply copy and paste—making it easy for people to tell their friends about Kiva. What's fascinating about their implementation is that it uses *no special*

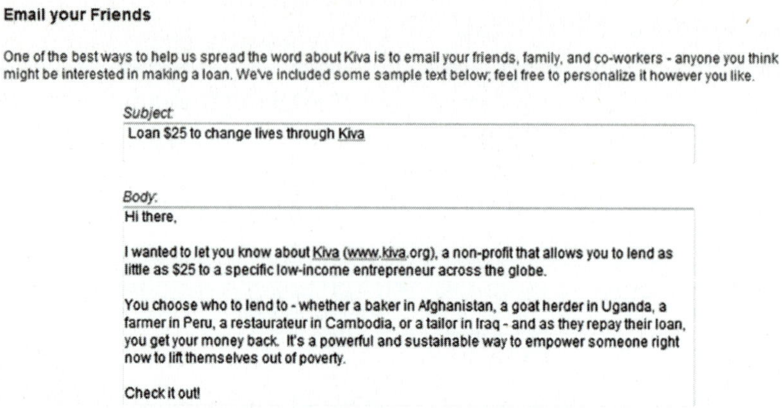

Email your Friends

One of the best ways to help us spread the word about Kiva is to email your friends, family, and co-workers - anyone you think might be interested in making a loan. We've included some sample text below; feel free to personalize it however you like.

Subject:

Loan $25 to change lives through Kiva

Body:

Hi there,

I wanted to let you know about Kiva (www.kiva.org), a non-profit that allows you to lend as little as $25 to a specific low-income entrepreneur across the globe.

You choose who to lend to - whether a baker in Afghanistan, a goat herder in Uganda, a farmer in Peru, a restaurateur in Cambodia, or a tailor in Iraq - and as they repay their loan, you get your money back. It's a powerful and sustainable way to empower someone right now to lift themselves out of poverty.

Check it out!

FIGURE 12.2 Screen Shot of Kiva's "Email Your Friends" Page

software. They kept it simple, but it accomplishes the goal (see Figure 12.2).

Kiva goes even further in getting help to spread their message. In addition to the ease of allowing people to e-mail their friends, Kiva also provides simple instructions on how to add the Kiva message to a person's e-mail signature. When a particularly loyal member of the community adds this message, every e-mail he or she sends out contains Kiva's message at the bottom of the e-mail.

For its more tech savvy community members, Kiva provides several ways to promote the organization on the web, the most impressive tactic being a dynamic banner/ad that users can add to their websites. Figure 12.3 shows an example.

We love this banner ad tactic for several reasons. Once the banner is installed on a website, the amount of traffic it generates for Kiva increases as that website grows, meaning Kiva is piggybacking on the success of its members' own websites. Second, the banner is *dynamic* and allows Kiva to show a specific call-to-action with a specific goal.

In addition to *building* their reach, Kiva also does a great job of *nurturing* that reach. For example, like many people, we were intrigued by the idea behind Kiva and registered right away. But, like many people, we didn't spend the time to go through the steps to actually make a loan due to becoming distracted with other things. A few days later, we received the following friendly e-mail from Kiva. (See Figure 12.4.)

FIGURE 12.3 Screen Shot of Kiva's Banner on Their website

This e-mail worked because it was clearly sent *only* to users that had registered for the site, but not actually completed a loan. The e-mail included a specific call-to-action: "I wanted to check in and invite you back to lend to an entrepreneur today." Third, Jessica recognizes that Dharmesh might not be ready to take the next step yet and offers more information and the ability to ask questions—*by responding to the*

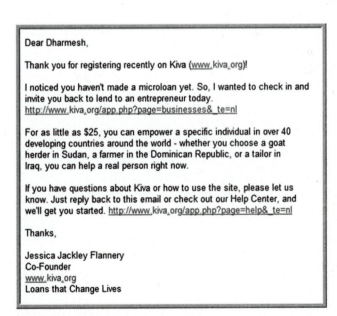

FIGURE 12.4 Kiva E-Mail Reminder to Registrant

e-mail! The entire message has a casual but professional tone. It's effective in stating Kiva's goals, but does not sell too hard and is one of the best examples of proper lead nurturing we've seen.

To Do

1. If you have dozens or hundreds of leads coming in, you should use the criteria above to grade them and then hand your qualified opportunities to your sales reps.
2. If you have dozens or hundreds of leads coming in, you should segment and nurture your unqualified opportunities until they are ready for your sales organization.
3. You should start measuring your market reach over time, including the number of e-mail addresses, blog subscribers, Twitter followers, LinkedIn group members, Facebook friends, and so on.

4. _____

5. _____

6. _____

Part IV

Make Better Decisions

In God we trust; all others bring data.

—*Dr. W. Edwards Deming*

Chapter 13

Make Better Marketing Decisions

If you're like many marketers, you already have a very long "to do" list: buying e-mail lists and sending out e-mail blasts, hiring tele-marketers, hiring/managing PR firms to call magazine editors about your press releases, managing and attending trade shows, developing marketing campaigns, and so on. If you want to run before you walk with inbound marketing, then you'll need to cross the least productive outbound marketing items off your to-do list and add a few of the new inbound marketing items (e.g., content creation), measure the results for a while (e.g., three to six months), and then continue to eliminate the least productive old-school tactics at the bottom and replace them with new and more productive channels/campaigns. After a year or so, much of your marketing to-do list will end up being inbound activities; on average, inbound marketing leads are 61 percent less expensive than outbound marketing leads.

How do you decide which "to-do's" to cross off and which to add? Your first step is to create a living, breathing sales and marketing funnel to help you make marketing investment decisions. The inputs at the top of the funnel include all of your channels/campaigns that drive leads into your business, such as e-mail marketing, trade shows, seminars, sales relationships, telemarketing, cold calls, branded organic search traffic (e.g., searchers who use your company name), unbranded search traffic (searchers who use industry terms), paid search traffic (if any), traffic from social media sites, and traffic from blogs and other websites, among others. These tactics all drive targeted and untargeted prospects into your funnel—and generally, not all of these prospects come out at the bottom as paying customers, which is why you must grade, qualify, and nurture your leads. We call it a funnel, rather than a pipeline, because it is shaped like a funnel—there are a lot more inputs coming in the top than customers coming out the bottom.

Levels and Definitions

The first step in creating your funnel is coming up with a list of sources/campaigns/inputs at the top of your funnel that create prospects for your products and services.

After you have determined which sources/campaigns/channels drive prospects into the top (prospect level) of your funnel, you then need to figure out a definition for the second step of your funnel. Let's call this the leads stage for lack of a better term. A lead might be anyone a salesperson (or you) qualifies as being eligible to spend at least an hour with, showing your product or discussing your service. After you have figured out the lead stage definition, you then determine the definition of the third stage of the funnel, which we'll call the opportunity stage. At this stage, the potential customer has an internal champion within a company advocating for a purchase of your company's product or service this quarter. The last level in the funnel is the "customer" step—someone who has purchased your product or service. The key is not to over-think this exercise—limit your team to a one-hour meeting to make decisions on the funnel stages and defini- tions. You can hire an outside consultant and spend hundreds of thousands of dollars to come up with funnel definitions, but you can do it yourself if you are decisive. The key to an effective sales funnel is not the decision criteria—it's that you have a funnel (see Figure 13.1) and that you consistently measure it.

Now that you have your levels (prospect, lead, opportunity, cus- tomer), you measure the size of each level on a quarterly (or monthly) basis. Once you have the size of each level, you can measure the conversion rate between each phase plus the total yield of the fun- nel—the percent of prospects that turn into customers (see Figure 13.2).

Campaign Yield

The key piece of information you get from this exercise is the shape (ratios) of the funnel per campaign/channel. For example, you might

FIGURE 13.1 Funnel Diagram

look at your branded organic search (people using your company name during a Google search) funnel. How many prospects last quarter did you get from branded organic search, how many leads did you get from that channel, how many opportunities, how many customers, and what was the overall yield (prospects over customers) of that channel? How did those numbers change relative to the previous quarter?

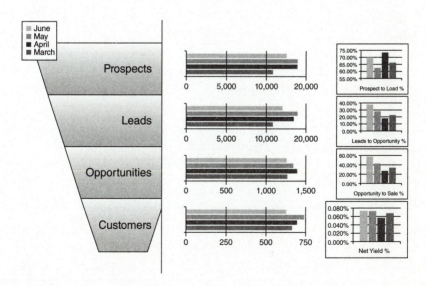

FIGURE 13.2 Funnel Metrics

You should also determine ROI (return on investment) per channel. For example, you can compare the cost per channel, per quarter, with the revenue that channel produced per quarter.

This campaign yield and ROI information should influence which items you cross off the bottom of your marketing to-do list, and which tactics should get additional resources. The better the yield and higher the ROI, the more resources you should pour into that channel. The low yield and low ROI campaigns should be replaced, *even if they are sacred cows*. A typical sacred cow is the annual trade show that "everyone" goes to, but never results in any business because "everyone" includes competitors and job-seekers, but not potential customers.

As this book is on inbound marketing, we suggest that once you get this framework in place, you cross off your bottom two channels and add two new inbound channels (e.g., a blog and Twitter).

Tracking Your Progress

This chapter is about measurement: measure your monthly prospects, leads, opportunities, and customers per channel over time as well as the ratios between the levels over time. Use this information to help you decide which programs to double down on and which to eliminate.

To Do

1. Define all of your marketing campaigns/channels.
2. Define your funnel stages.
3. Measure each stage by channel.
4. Measure the yield by channel.
5. Measure the ROI by channel.
6. Replace poor performing outbound channels with new inbound channels.
7. _____
8. _____
9. _____

Chapter **14**

Picking and Measuring Your People

The rules of marketing haven't changed much since companies such as Procter & Gamble, Coca-Cola, and IBM perfected the craft of interrupting their way into customers' minds and wallets using outbound marketing. As we have shown throughout this book, the era of interruption-based marketing is waning because people have become much more efficient at blocking out these traditional methods of marketing and have become equally as efficient at finding *trusted* information online.

The next several decades will usher in an era of inbound marketing. Just as P&G, Coca-Cola, and IBM built huge companies because they became really good at interruptive marketing, a new wave of successful companies will be built around inbound marketing. Will one of those companies be yours?

What does this change mean for your marketing staff? Simply put, your hiring criteria needs to change and your way of measuring performance needs to change along with it. The following is a suggested framework, called DARC, for hiring and developing inbound marketing savvy employees.

D = Hire **D**igital Citizens

A = Hire for **A**nalytical Chops

R = Hire for Web **R**each

C = Hire **C**ontent Creators

Hire Digital Citizens

Do you know people who happen to be handy around the house and who are as good with wrenches and pipes as they are with saws and wood? You know, the people that just feel *comfortable* around tools and can get things done. Maybe they were born with that gene (which neither of the authors were) or maybe they just acquired that skillset over time. However they got there, they are *at home* in this environment.

We think the web is similar in that way. Some people seem to really "get" the Internet and are naturally curious about it and others aren't. Instead of being digital *tourists* who are just passing through and will take in a site here or there—they are digital *citizens*. They are *committed* to the Internet—they are comfortable on the web and *live there* for some portion of their lives.

In this new era of inbound marketing, it's important that you hire Digital Citizens, not Digital Tourists. It's relatively hard to figure this out using standard interview questions, so you need to test for it. Your marketing interviews should include questions like the following:

♦ What blogs do you read?
♦ How do you keep up with news and happenings?
♦ Do you rank first for your name in Google?
♦ Do you have a blog? Can you show it to me?
♦ Do you use Facebook or LinkedIn? When was the last time you updated your profile?
♦ Do you use Twitter? Can you show me?
♦ Do you have a channel on YouTube? Can you show it to me?

If your prospective hire gives you blank stares or a lot of "I was planning on setting that up," then you don't have a Digital Citizen on your hands.

Hire for Analytical Chops

The good thing about inbound marketing is that so many things are now *measureable*. No longer do you have arguments about how XYZ or ABC major account found your product. You know whether it was a

Google search (and which term the customer used), a link from another site, a discussion on LinkedIn Groups, or others. The old saying, "I know I'm wasting half my marketing budget, but I'm just not sure which half" is no longer true in the inbound marketing era.

Modern marketing organizations must analyze all of this great information in order to make better decisions. This means that when you bring on new hires, some of them should be very Analytical. It's difficult to figure out if someone is Analytical from a standard interview, so to test for it, you should have your prospective hire bring to the interview his or her favorite spreadsheet with pivot tables, and show you some counterintuitive insight that came out of the spreadsheet model in graph format.

You could also have a couple of sample spreadsheets that you use in your own organization. Ask the candidate to look them over and let them ask you questions. Your objective is not to "stump" them—it's to determine how they think about things. Do they take this data and try to *analyze* for patterns and lessons? Do they try to draw out insights? Even if the insight is wrong, that's okay—it's their mental process you're trying to figure out).

Hire for Their Web Reach

Over the years, it has been common practice for companies to hire sales representatives who have a Rolodex full of contacts in their industries—their contacts can help them short circuit the sales process. In the era of inbound marketing, it's become just as important for marketers to have a Rolodex, but not the same type of Rolodex as a salesperson's. This new type of Rolodex is called Web Reach.

Good inbound marketers today are cultivating their own personal network of loose (e.g., blog subscribers, Twitter followers) and tight (e.g., Facebook friends) connections within their industries through the web. Good inbound marketers often have their own blogs, Twitter feeds, Facebook accounts, LinkedIn accounts, and so on. Just as we discussed earlier in the book about corporate reach, individual inbound marketers, too, have Reach. If you hire a marketer within your industry who has a large Twitter following or a popular industry blog, your company dramatically extends its reach because that marketer opens up new channels into the top of your funnel.

Similar to the other inbound marketing criteria, Reach is a little difficult to tease out in a typical interview, so you should do some online research about the candidate, and ask pointed questions when you are both in front of a computer during the interview—yes, marketing interviews should include a session where you and the interviewee are online together. The following are some of the questions you might ask to determine if potential new hires have significant web Reach:

- ◆ How many subscribers to your blog do you have? Do you talk about our industry on your blog or about personal stuff?
- ◆ How many Facebook followers do you have? Do you talk about our industry at all on your Facebook account?
- ◆ How many Twitter followers do you have? Do you talk about our industry on your Twitter account?
- ◆ Have you been participating in any online professional communities for marketing, like inbound.org?

Compare a prospective hire's Reach to that of other candidates and your company's own reach to see if you can open up the top of your funnel by bringing this person on board.

Web reach is relatively hard to acquire and is very valuable. Most organizations underestimate both of these assets. If you can become skilled at evaluating an individual's Reach, you'll be able to snap up some high-quality talent that is relatively undervalued in the marketplace. Eventually, all companies will figure this out, so there is a short-term window for you to take advantage of the situation.

A great example of a company that understands the value of web reach and is actively recruiting for it is American Express. They recently had the brilliant idea of hiring Guy Kawasaki to start writing for them on the American Express blog. Guy is an author, entrepreneur (alltop.com), and investor who was an early blogger about these topics, and because of his *remark*able content, he's built up a huge following, including over 70,000 blog followers and over 1.4 million twitter followers. Most of Guy's new, *remark*able blog content is now written for American Express. In addition to American Express getting great content, Guy posts a note on his blog (see Figure 14.1) and on Twitter pointing his 1.4 million-plus subscriber/followers to the American Express blog. American Express is greatly benefitting from Guy Kawasaki's reach!

	LinkedIn Followers	Twitter Grader	Facebook Group	Blog Subscribers
Jane CEO	200	0	10	0
Joe CMO	300	80	50	0
Marvin PR	400	90	60	10
Linda Marketing	500	99	90	3000

FIGURE 14.1   Guy Kawasaki's Reach Being Leveraged by American Express

Hire Content Creators

As we have discussed, inbound marketing starts with creating *remark-able* content that spreads virally in social media, attracts links from other sites, and drives up your rankings in Google. This remarkable content turns your website from a small town like Wellesley, Massachusetts (one highway), to a large metropolis like New York City (many high-ways, many airports, many train stations, many bus depots).

Your next marketing hire, therefore, should be someone with great writing skills, preferably an existing journalist looking to make a career change, rather than a technical writer of manuals. Before hiring this person, we recommend you test them by paying them (approximately $200) to write a blog article for you. You should measure the effectiveness of this article by seeing how many links it attracted, how many views it got, and how many comments it received relative to other blog content you have produced.

Another interesting skill to have in-house is someone who can create remarkable video content for you. If you want to stick your toe in the water with video, you could hire an intern from a local university who is majoring in film or interactive media or use someone internally who has basic technical skills. You can buy this person a video camera for $250 and send him or her off to work. If you want to test potential recruits for aptitude, just ask them to show you other videos they have made and have posted to YouTube.

Developing Existing Marketers

Many professional marketers today are so steeped in the traditions and skill sets of old-school, outbound marketing that it can be difficult to get them to learn new skills. It's very hard to teach someone to be analytical or to become a good content creator if they're not trained that way early on, but you can make an attempt at improving people's inbound marketing knowledge. You can send people to the INBOUND conference (http://inbound.com) or attend the virtual HubSpot Academy and get a free certification for inbound marketing. You could even point them to this book. Finally, you could send them to http://inbound.org—a free community that we built *specifically* to help a million marketers learn, grow, and connect.

A great way to tell who your future stars will be is by seeing how they *react* to all this new information and opportunity. If they fight it every step of the way, it's likely going to be a tough transition. But you will find a few who enthusiastically welcome the new learning and embrace the resources you point them to with open arms.

Tracking Your Progress

In baseball, a "five-tooled" player is one who can field, throw, hit for average, hit for power, and steal bases—an ideal player! In inbound marketing, an ideal hire is a "four-tooled" player: a Digital Citizen who is Analytical, has web Reach, and who can Create *remark*able content. Will it be easy to find D, A, R, and C in spades? Probably not—there just are not a lot of them around yet! If you have a very small business, then you want to try to get as many of these qualities in one person as you can. If you are in a slightly larger business, you can specialize a bit by hiring some folks who are analytical and others who are content creators as an example.

If you are like most companies, you do not have a huge budget to go out and hire lots of new people, so it pays to have more of your current team do some of the work. Some of these skills are hard to measure (e.g., Analytical), but others are easy to measure. We suggest you create a Reach Grader grid for your organization, where you track your executives' and your marketers' individual Reach and how it changes over time. See Table 14.1 for a good example. The Reach Grader is the type of tool that should be updated and posted on a monthly basis. All of this information is public, so you might as well pull it together and let all employees consume it on an ongoing basis. It will create a strong incentive to improve.

On the content creation side, you should track each piece of content's impact on the funnel. For example, if you have two people

TABLE **14.1**   Reach Grader Grid Measuring Employees' Web Reach

	LinkedIn Followers	Twitter Followers	Facebook Fans	Blog Subscribers
Jane—CEO	200	0	10	0
Joe—CMO	300	80	50	0
Marvin—PR	400	4,000	300	1,000
Linda—Marketing	500	1,500	210	3,000

TABLE **14.2**   Marketing Grader for Employees

	Digital Citizen	Analytical	Reach	Content Creation	Score
Joe—CMO	2	8	2	1	13
Marvin—PR	5	7	3	5	20
Linda—Marketing	7	2	8	7	24

writing blog content, you should track which person's articles drew in more new visitors who ultimately ended up buying your products or service. This is the type of information that should be publicly available in your company—the mere act of making it public will create incentive for improvement.

In terms of how to evaluate marketers in their annual reviews, you might think of creating a different model similar to the one in Table 14.2 (Marketing Grader), where you and your peers rate each employee on a scale of 1 to 10 for each inbound marketing criterion. The Reach and Content creation columns can be derived squarely from the data, while the analytical and Digital Citizen data are a bit more subjective.

Each company is a little bit different, so we suspect you'll want to add other criteria to the list along with the ones listed below—perhaps some of the items from Jack Welch's leadership 4E's might be good additions.

What gets measured gets done. If you track these inbound marketing criteria and tie them to raises, promotions, and recognition, you'll develop a competitive advantage for your company over time.

Inbound in Action: Jack Welch and GE

We've always been big fans of legendary General Electric CEO Jack Welch. Jack ran GE for 30 years, during which time he increased the value of the business 30 times and turned it into the most valuable company on the planet. In Jack's books and lectures (he is a senior lecturer at MIT these days), he credits much of his success with his hiring/evaluation criteria for his employees. Jack spent 50 percent of his time on talent acquisition, evaluation, and development. He had four criteria he used for evaluating talent at GE:

1. Energy—Individuals with energy love to "go, go, go." These people possess boundless energy and get up every day ready to attack the job at hand. High-energy people move at 95 miles per hour in a 55-mile-per-hour world.

2. Energizers—These people know how to spark others to perform. They outline a vision and get people to carry it out. Energizers know how to get others excited about a cause or crusade. They are selfless in giving others the credit when things go right, but are quick to accept responsibility when things go awry.

3. Edge—People with edge are competitive types. They know how to make the really difficult decisions, such as hiring, firing, and promoting, never allowing the degree of difficulty to stand in their way.

4. Execute—This is the key to the entire model. Without measurable results, the other E's are of little use. Executers recognize that activity and productivity are not the same and are capable of converting energy and edge into action and results.

Just as Jack Welch spent much of his time recruiting talent, evaluating performance, and developing performance using his 4E's, we recommend you use the DARC criteria to evaluate potential marketing recruits, evaluate marketing employee performance, and develop your staff. Because we are at the beginning of the inbound marketing era, getting people in your company who possess these characteristics, evaluating them along these criteria, and developing these qualities can give you a competitive advantage. Five years from now, everyone will be looking for inbound marketing mavens, so now is the time to put these people in place and develop your existing people along these lines.

To Do

1. Increase the percentage of time you allocate to recruiting, evaluating, and developing inbound marketing mavens.
2. When hiring new marketers, use the DARC criteria: Digital Citizen, Analytical, web Reach, and Content creation.
3. Evaluate yourself, your staff, and executives using the Reach Grader. Show changes over time.
4. Measure your staff over time using the Marketing Grader. Tie improvement to compensation.
5. _____
6. _____
7. _____

Chapter 15

Picking and Measuring a PR Agency

Traditionally, a PR agency earns its fees by introducing its clients to editors of print journals that cover their industry, such as *CIO Magazine* or *Modern Bride*. This model has been beneficial for the PR firms, clients, and print journalists for several decades now.

PR agencies have two core competencies. They have a network of relationships with print media people *and* they are efficient at interrupting print media people in an attempt to get your new offerings in front of them. However, both of these core competencies have problems.

The first problem is that the print journalists no longer have a corner on the market for news as more people turn to bloggers and social media for critical information. The interesting thing that has happened is we have gone from a world where there were a limited number of journalists whom a PR agency needed to have relationships with to a world where everyone is a journalist. In the inbound marketing era, it is nearly impossible for a PR firm to have proprietary relationships with all of the key journalists and influencers in an industry—let alone multiple industries.

The second problem is that information is much more readily available to journalists and bloggers, so they no longer rely on PR firms to funnel it to them. Just as your customers are getting better at blocking out interruptions, journalists and bloggers are getting better at blocking out interruptions from PR firms.

In this inbound marketing era, does the PR agency still have its place? Well, it depends on your company and on the PR firm you are dealing with.

If your company is full of four-tooled players who are Digital Citizens, Analytical, have huge Reach, and are Content creators, then you might not get maximum value from a PR agency. This is particularly true about the reach criteria. If your company has some holes to fill, particularly in the reach area, then you could end up getting great value from the right type of PR agency.

Picking a PR Agency

There are a number of filters you should use when selecting a PR agency.

The first filter piggybacks on the digital citizen and reach criteria from the previous chapter. When you meet with a PR firm, you typically meet a partner who is a fantastic salesperson. Once you are on the path to a decision, you meet the team that actually works with you; these people are typically much less experienced than the partner. You should evaluate the partner, and each person on the team assigned to you, through Twitter and Facebook; look them up in LinkedIn; see if they rank first for their names in Google; and run their blogs through Website Grader. If you find that some of them are engaged less in the web than your own people, then you should probably keep looking. If you find a weak link, you might suggest it be replaced.

CARL DECIDES TO VISIT HIS NEXT-GENERATION PR CONSULTING FIRM IN-PERSON.

The second filter is to see whether the PR agency drinks its own champagne. You should run the PR agency's website through Website Grader. Many PR people will talk about how they focus on their customers and ignore their own sites when you bring up their Website Grade, or they will say they were just starting an initiative to begin inbound marketing for their own agencies. Our advice is to *not* buy either of these arguments. If they really understood inbound marketing, they would find the time to better market themselves.

Third, ask the prospective PR agency for the names of some of their other clients and how long their clients have been with them. Run their clients through Website Grader and note their clients' Website Grades relative to your own, and take particular note of the inbound links section and compare it to your own.

By running these three simple filters on your PR agency or prospective PR agency, you avoid getting sold by the one person in the firm who actually gets this stuff, and then being moved to the rest of the firm once you sign up. The good news is that the PR industry is full of smart people and they realize the industry is transforming, so more firms can pass these filters.

Tracking Your Progress

Once you have a PR agency, you can use many complicated and expensive tools for measuring them. We give you two simple ways to measure success.

First, you want to measure the number of new links into your site and the number of new websites linking to yours. Once you hire a PR firm, you should see the number of websites linking to your website increase in pace. This increase sends you more traffic and helps you improve your Google rankings. If you want specific bloggers and websites to link to you, then you should make a list of those sites and have your PR agency track how many of them link to you on a monthly basis. If you are not seeing a material increase in the number of sites linking to your site, you have a problem with your PR firm. If you are seeing a big increase in the number of links, your PR agency should be rewarded.

The second thing you want to measure is the number of mentions your brand(s) is getting in Google when you do a search on it and you

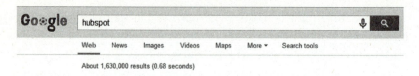

FIGURE **15.1**   Brand Mentions in Google

should track this metric over time. (See Figure 15.1.) If your brand is not getting mentioned at increasing rates in Google, then you have an issue with your PR agency. If your brand is increasingly mentioned in Google, your PR agency should be rewarded.

Inbound in Action: Solis, Weber, Defren & Roetzer

A handful of PR professionals out there really get it, judging by their own reach, the improved reach of their clients, and the content they are producing. Here are a few examples.

Brian Solis at FutureWorks maintains a blog called bub.blicio.us and another one called PR2.0, which both got website grades of 97, meaning they are authoritative. In addition, Brian has over 218,000 Twitter followers. "Inbound marketing versus outbound marketing is the difference between broadcast PR and genuine "public relations," says Solis. "PR agencies, consultants, and communications professionals either establish an epicenter that serves as the resource hub for their industry or they will intentionally remove themselves from the radar screens of customers and influencers alike. In the social web, we are presented with a privilege to establish meaningful dialogue and collaborative relationships with the people who define our markets. This is an incredible opportunity to establish relevance and discoverability. Remember, consumers have choices. We're not part of those decisions where we're not present. Inbound marketing serves as the bridge between those seeking information, direction, and insight and those willing to provide guidance and support." Solis clearly understands how to create content, optimize that content, and market it to create a following. Having him in your corner brings you expertise and some reach.

Larry Weber at W2 Group published a book called *Marketing to the Social Web*, which is about how to build and leverage customer communities. It is less about leveraging inbound marketing to get found by your customers and more about leveraging your existing customer community. According to Larry, "Inbound marketing is the right approach in the 'dialogue age' of marketing and hits the bulls-eye on the future of customer-centric relationships."

Todd Defren at Shift Communications maintains a blog called PR-Squared that scored a 99 on Website Grader. Todd has over 25,000 followers on Twitter. According to Todd, "Inbound Marketing is find-ability based on authority based on authenticity based on content based on passion."

Paul Roetzer runs PR20/20, an inbound marketing agency. His firm has a unique business model that allows companies to buy inbound marketing PR a la carte. "Inbound Marketing has given PR firms the ability to expand their service offerings and consistently deliver measurable results, including: inbound links, website traffic, leads, and sales. There is tremendous demand developing for social-media savvy agencies that can build relationships, produce search engine optimized content, and directly impact the bottom line."

These four people get inbound marketing and have reach. The question you need to ask yourself is whether they are a good fit for your business. You also need to figure out if the people you currently work with really understand inbound marketing, or whether just the founders who create the content are the ones who actually understand it.

To Do

1. Evaluate whether you really need a PR agency.
2. Pick a PR agency by running them through the three simple filters discussed earlier.
3. Measure a PR agency by running them through the two simple filters discussed earlier.

4. _____

5. _____

6. _____

Chapter 16

Watching Your Competition

We recently spent some time with Jim Cash. Jim is a former professor at Harvard Business School and now is a professional board member, serving on the boards of Microsoft, GE, Walmart, Chubb, and the Boston Celtics, among others.

We asked Jim to tell us about some of the world-class CEOs with whom he has worked. He mentioned a few attributes about them, but the one that stuck out was that the top CEOs were all a little bit paranoid. They were always watching what their competitors were doing and were all leery of potential upstarts that could do damage to them. What Jim had to say is consistent with what legendary Intel CEO Andy Grove said in his book titled *Only the Paranoid Survive*.

The web is a flattener of all marketplaces—it is the ultimate meritocracy. Because the web makes it so much more efficient to spread ideas, it poses a great opportunity for upstarts with unique new products or services, so you should be more paranoid now than you have ever been because you have never been so vulnerable!

Tools to Keep Tabs on Competitors

On the flip side, it is easier than ever to track how your competition is doing on the web if you know what you are doing. Here are six different ways you can track yourself relative to your competitors:

1. Website Grade—Go to Grader.com and run your website alongside your competitors' websites to see how well you do. Pay special attention to upstart competitors who might

be more focused on leveraging the web than some of the more traditional players.

2. Inbound Links—Look on the Grader report and pull out the number of links for you and your competitors. An increase in the number of links to a site can indicate that a competitor is getting more traction with its products.

3. Facebook Fans—Go to Facebook.com and see the number of fans your company's website has relative to your competitor's website. You will have to search around to find the company page in Facebook. This number is worth tracking over time—if your competitor starts to gain a lot of fans, then it means their customer loyalty is increasing. This might mean it is going to get harder to steal customers from them, forcing you to focus on non-consuming parts of your market.

4. Compete—Go to Compete.com and compare their estimate of the traffic your site is getting versus your competitors.

5. SiteAlerts—Go to SiteAlerts.com and see what number of mentions you're getting on the web, and what keywords are driving search traffic. Compare that to your competitors.

6. Buzz—Go to Google and do a search on "your brand" (in quotations) and look at the number of results in the upper right-hand corner. Do the same for each of your competitors. The number of results shows the number of pages on the web where the brand is mentioned. This metric is worth tracking over time as it will let you know how your "buzz" is relative to your competitors'. You can do the same thing in blogsearch .google.com to see how your buzz is going relative to your competitors in the blogosphere.

Tracking Your Progress

The following is a snapshot of the tool we use to track how we are doing on these important metrics relative to our competitors (see Figure 16.1). We recommend you track your traditional competitors, upstarts, and companies you consider as alternatives to your product.

It is important to get a baseline of how you are doing relative to your competitors once, but even more important to get a baseline of how

WEBSITE	WEBSITE GRADE	GOOGLE PAGE RANK	TRAFFIC RANK	BLOG RANK	INBOUND LINKS	DEL.ICIO.US BOOKMARKS	GOOGLE INDEXED PAGES	KEYWORDS IN GOOGLE TOP 100
www.hubspot.com	99	6	8,911	3,224	37,538	930	551	701
www.websitegrader.com	93	6	184,416	Not Ranked	37,819	4,685	83	8
blog.hubspot.com	99	5	8,871	8,078	33,179	228	921	353
twitter.grader.com	99	5	4,734	3,233	230,240	2,209	63,000	58

FIGURE 16.1   Competitor Grader

you are doing relative to your competitors over time. (See Figure 16.2.) You need to look at each of these metrics and watch for big moves along any of these dimensions. As mentioned earlier, the web can give competitors a big advantage if they know how to use it.

Inbound in Action: TechTarget

TechTarget was founded in 1999 and went public in 2007. TechTarget is an expert at using inbound marketing to generate leads that it sells to technology companies. They create topic-specific websites with *remark*able content that draw people in, and develop leads that they then sell to technology companies. According to Greg Strakosch,

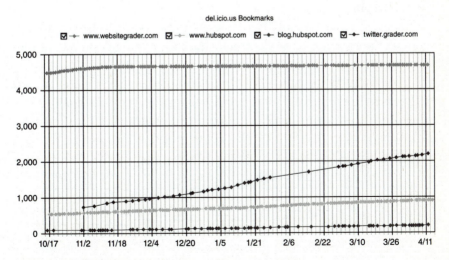

FIGURE 16.2   Delicious Bookmark Comparison Over Time

WEBSITE	WEBSITE GRADE	GOOGLE PAGE RANK	TRAFFIC RANK	BLOG RANK	INBOUND LINKS	DEL.ICIO.US BOOKMARKS	GOOGLE INDEXED PAGES	KEYWORDS IN GOOGLE TOP 100
constructionsoftwarereview.com	90	5	513,171	1,815,794	6,344	7	3,560	765
searchcrm.techtarget.com	95	6	1,993	Not Ranked	13,051	59	8,020	N/A
www.nationalcontractors.com	84	4	577,845	Not Ranked	8,898	9	12,700	N/A
www.distributionsoftwarereview.com	23	1	8,716,642	Not Ranked	42	1	80	N/A
www.gantthead.com	89	6	87,720	137,757	23,727	958	21,400	N/A
project-management-software.org	57	5	205,022	Not Ranked	714	218	75	N/A
www.web-based-software.com	67	5	239,568	Not Ranked	2,031	119	269	N/A
www.findaccountingsoftware.com	89	5	234,390	Not Ranked	2,398	20	20,100	N/A
www.healthtechnologyreview.com	90	4	799,498	7,603	1,666	12	572	N/A

FIGURE 16.3 TechTarget Comparison Chart

founder and CEO of TechTarget, "Our use of inbound marketing techniques has been a key ingredient in our success thus far."

Like a lot of successful companies, they are very clever about how they analyze their competition and how they analyze each site relative to that of their peers. Figure 16.3 shows how they lay it out for themselves.

For each one of those web metrics, they then track how they are doing versus their competitors and peers over time, as is shown here, where they look at their Website Grade for constructionsoftwarereview.com (moved from last to first) relative to their competition over time (see Figure 16.4).

They also like to analyze how they are doing relative to their competition/peers in Google organic rankings, and keep track of it in the following tool (see Figure 16.5).

Strakosch commented, "All of this competitive information is used to keep us abreast of how we are doing against the competition. It is also used in our sales cycle to differentiate us from the competition."

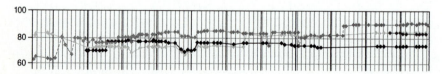

FIGURE 16.4 TechTarget Historic Comparison

KEYWORD	MONTHLY SEARCHES	CONSTRUCTION... RANK	SOFTWAREADVI... RANK	CAPTERRA RANK	CTSGUIDES RANK
applied computer systems jobpower review	Low	1	100+	100+	3
applied computer systems review	Low	1	100+	100+	49
builderhelper review	Low	1	100+	100+	100+

FIGURE 16.5 TechTarget SEO Comparison

To Do

1. Be more paranoid.
2. Run your site through the different tools described earlier.
3. Track the results in a spreadsheet or application.
4. Track the results over time and check on a monthly basis.
5. _____
6. _____

Chapter 17

On Commitment, Patience, and Learning

L earning inbound marketing is like learning to play the guitar. The first step in playing the guitar is learning how to play the G chord by placing three fingers on your left hand in awkward positions and strumming the strings with a pick in your right hand. The second step is learning the C chord and the D chord, both of which involve tricky three finger positions on the left hand and strumming with a pick in the right hand. The third step is learning to move your left hand between these three chords quickly. The fourth step is doing a strum with your right hand that sounds half decent while you are moving between the three chords on your left hand. The fifth step is finally learning your first simplistic song. In any given year, x number of people take up learning how to play guitar; $.5x$ get to step 2, $.25x$ get to step 3, $.125x$ get to step 4, and $.06x$ get to step 5. In other words, for every 100 people who start to play guitar, only six get through the first hurdles to play a simplistic song. Up until step 5, the hours you spend practicing are most ungratifying because everything you do sounds terrible. Once you get to step 5, it becomes easier to play and you get immediate gratification from practicing more. In other words, there is a big hurdle at the beginning of learning to play guitar and this hurdle weeds out those people who are not fully committed. Once you get over the barrier, however, the benefits accrue quickly in a most satisfying way.

Learning to do inbound marketing has a small hump in the learning curve in a similar way as learning to play the guitar does. In order to get maximum value from inbound marketing in the form of leads, you need to stick your leg in the water for a couple of months to start, not stick your toe in the water for a couple of days. The benefits come very slowly at first, but they accumulate until you reach successive tipping points. For example, if you just start writing a blog, you do not get much benefit. If you write a blog and your company builds a large following in Twitter, then you get much more benefit from every blog article you write, as you can spread your blog articles through your Twitter network ($1 + 1 = 3$).

You'll come to points in this process where you'll want to give up, and only those who persevere will make it through. The reality is that none of these individual steps is all that difficult, but they take perseverance.

If you have not started doing inbound marketing yet, get started today before your competitors do. If you have dipped your toe in the water and haven't seen results, put your whole leg in. We have seen inbound marketing work firsthand for hundreds of companies in a myriad of different industries—we're confident it will work for you if you persevere and continually learn.

Tracking Your Progress

Go to your calendar and physically block out some time every day of the week for the next three months, during which you will create remarkable content, optimize that content for search engines and social media, publish that content, market the content through social media, and measure the results.

Inbound in Action: Tom Brady

Tom Brady was a backup quarterback at the University of Michigan for his first two years before becoming a starting quarterback later in his career. He was drafted by the New England Patriots in the sixth round after 199 other players, and made the team initially as its fourth-string backup quarterback. When their All-Pro starter, Drew Bledsoe, went down with an injury, Coach Bill Belichick put in Tom Brady. The rest is history, with Brady going on to break the all-time touchdown record for one season and leading the Patriots to three Super Bowl victories (so far).

When interviewed about Tom Brady, Coach Belichick said Brady did not have the physical attributes of a great quarterback in those early years, but he practiced harder than anyone else on the team. In fact, when the coach would arrive at practice, Brady would already be there, having organized the practice squad to do extra drills before the regular squad arrived. Brady persevered despite sitting on the bench behind an All-Pro quarterback for what must have seemed like an eternity.

The great thing about inbound marketing is that you don't have to be a diamond in the rough like Tom Brady. Although social media does take some time, creativity, and know-how, it also has very low barriers to entry—meaning anyone can do it as long you persevere and commit to it. Keep working away at it, and before long you'll find yourself a minor celebrity in your extended network.

To Do

1. Open your calendar and book two hours a day for the next three months to dedicate to getting found, converting, and making better decisions using inbound marketing.

2. Start summarizing your "to do" lists from this book.

3. _____

4. _____

5. _____

6. _____

Chapter 18

Why Now?

One hundred years ago, most companies were local businesses and most of their marketing happened door-to-door. The introduction of motion pictures, radio, and television platforms ushered in the first major marketing shift in the last century as companies found it much more efficient to do mass outbound marketing to consumers and businesses. Because outbound marketing scaled better nationally than locally, this new, efficient marketing model enabled companies to became national in footprint. Companies such as P&G, Budweiser, and McDonald's, as well as the major Madison Avenue firms that were masters of efficiently converting huge sums of money into even more valuable customer relationships through outbound marketing, grew into the behemoths they are today.

This outbound marketing revolution has lasted for more than 50 years, and is winding down as people become more efficient at blocking marketing interruptions and turn instead to the web for their learning and shopping needs. This seismic shift in the way commerce takes place is giving rise to a whole new set of large companies, as well as a new type of Madison Avenue. The new companies and marketing/ PR firms will need to learn the new rules of inbound marketing in order to convert creativity, content, and conversation into valuable customers.

Just as the rules from door-to-door didn't translate to outbound mass marketing, the rules from outbound marketing do not apply to inbound marketing. You can't simply move your advertising budget and 30-second TV spot online—it won't work. Pushing a message at a potential customer when that message has not been requested will fail as a major source of new customers, and by extension, revenue, for most companies.

The churn rate of the Fortune 500 shows early evidence of this new seismic shift in the economic landscape. From 1955 until 1995, the average annual churn rate of the Fortune 500 was 4 percent. In other words, every year about 20 new companies dropped out of the Fortune 500 and 20 new companies entered. Since 1995, the churn rate has doubled to 8 percent per year—40 new companies drop out and 40 new companies enter. Of the 500 companies in the Fortune 500 in 1995, only 250 remained in 2009! The reshaping of the industrial landscape has already begun: New companies such as Amazon, eBay, and Google have joined the Fortune 500 and stalwarts such as Toys "R" Us, Ace Hardware, and Polaroid have left.

Seismic shifts like the one we're living through pose an amazing opportunity for new entrants into markets and an amazing threat to incumbent leaders (see Figure 18.1). New companies in markets with remarkable offerings can easily take advantage of the changing landscape to rise to the top. Old stalwarts relying on marketing techniques that worked in the 1960s will become vulnerable to attack.

FIGURE 18.1   Inbound Marketing Levels the Playing Field

Another interesting aspect of these shifts is that in these new markets, there tends to be one winner and several "also-rans." A few examples:

- ◆ eBay is number one in online auctions . . . who is number two?
- ◆ Google has 70+ percent of the search market.
- ◆ Zappos is number one in online shoes . . . who is number two?
- ◆ Amazon is number one in books . . . who is number two?
- ◆ Salesforce.com dominates the CRM (customer relationship management) business.

Will you take advantage of the shift from outbound to inbound to become the winner in your market? If so, now is the time to start, because if you wait another year or two, more of your competitors will have entered into your market, making it even more difficult for you to "catch up." You have in your hands the playbook for "getting found" by your prospective customers and have no reason not get started . . . now, today, this minute.

We hope this book changes how you do business. Inbound marketing has definitely changed how we do ours.

Tools and Resources

In this Appendix, we look at some of the tools and resources that we think you'll find useful as an inbound marketer.

Inbound.org

If you want to continue learning about inbound marketing and connect with others, a great place to visit is http://inbound.org.

This is an online community with tens of thousands of members all looking to share the best inbound marketing content available on the Internet—and to discuss, collaborate, and connect.

The site is free to join and is a great way to further your education and start building your professional reputation as an inbound marketer.

The site has a number of areas that you might find interesting and useful:

Jobs Board: A directory of jobs available in the inbound marketing industry. Posted by other community members.

Member Directory: A listing of all the members in the community, searchable by location, company name, and other keywords.

Event Directory: A list of upcoming marketing events including webinars, conferences, informal meet-ups, and online gatherings.

Tools Directory: A list of some of the most popular tools and technologies for marketers.

Advanced Google Search

You already know how to use Google. You use it every day. So you're probably thinking, "How can Google be a power tool for inbound marketers?" Chances are, you're not using Google to its fullest and some small tips can help a lot. The following are simple but powerful features to help you use Google.

If you're like most people, you simply type a search term into Google in the simplest way possible. You hope to get what you're looking for, and if you don't, well, you simply change the words. However, in addition to typing regular search queries, you can also use special modifiers that tell Google more about what you're looking for. Here are some of the most useful modifiers:

Explicit Phrase: Let's say you are looking for content about Internet marketing. Instead of just typing *Internet marketing* into the Google search box, you will likely be better off searching explicitly for the phrase. To do this, simply enclose the search phrase within double quotes.

Example: "Internet marketing"

Exclude Words: If you want to search for content about Internet marketing, but you want to exclude any results that contain the term *advertising*, simply use the "-" (hyphen) in front of the word you want to exclude.

Example Search: Internet marketing-advertising

Site Specific Search: Often, you want to search a specific website for content that matches a certain phrase. Even if the site doesn't support a built-in search feature, you can use Google to search the site for your term. Simply use the "site:somesite.com" modifier.

Example: "Internet marketing" site:inboundmarketing.com

Another useful tool that's a variation on this is to not include *any* keywords in the search, but just the "site:" operator. This tells you approximately how many pages from the specified site are in the Google index.

Example: site:www.facebook.com

Similar Words and Synonyms: If you want to include a word in your search, and also want to include results that contain similar words or synonyms, use the "~" (tilde) in front of the word.

Example: "Internet marketing" ~professional

Specific Document Types: If you're looking to find results that are of a specific type, you can use the modifier "filetype:". For example, you might want to find only PowerPoint presentations related to Internet marketing.

Example: "Internet marketing" filetype:pptx

This OR That: By default, when you do a search, Google will include all the terms specified in the search. If you are looking for one or more terms to match, then you can use the OR operator. (Note: The OR has to be capitalized.)

Example: Internet marketing OR advertising

Tracking with Site Alerts

Imagine if you had a personal assistant that did nothing but monitor the Internet for you. You'd hand him a list of websites (perhaps a list of your top competitors), and he'd dutifully type them into Google every day. Anytime something interesting showed up, he'd e-mail you. Even better, he'd remember which items he'd already sent you, so you only got the new stuff. That's precisely what Site Alerts does. And it's free!

To sign up for Site Alerts, visit http://SiteAlerts.com. Set up an account. Once your account is set up, adding alerts is easy. You enter the name of a website that is of interest (usually your own plus a couple of competitors).

BONUS: Entrepreneur's Guide to Startup Marketing

If you are thinking about a new startup, already have one, or are just planning on starting a new project, there are a number of tips that we'd suggest. The following list has been pulled together from years of experience at starting new things. Although the list is not comprehensive, it captures some of our best thinking in terms of actionable items.

Startup Marketing Checklist

If we were starting a new company or project today, these are the things we'd do in the first couple of weeks.

1. **Pick a name that will work long-term.** Needs to be simple, memorable, and unambiguous. The ".com" domain should be available without playing tricks with the name (like dropping vowels or adding dashes). Also, just because there's no website on a domain doesn't mean it's available. Available means something you can register immediately, or that has a price attached to it that you're willing to pay. Don't wander down the rabbit hole of finding the perfect name if you have no indication that it's for sale. This will waste a bunch of your time. See the next section for more tips on picking a name.

2. **Put up a simple website.** Doesn't have to be fancy. The goal is to put enough content on the site to start the Google clock. Don't worry about the site not saying much (nobody's going to be looking at it anyway). Make sure to use a decent content management system (CMS). If changing your web page involves uploading files via FTP—or a call to a friend or family member —you're doing it wrong. Even if you have technical skills, just because you can handcraft HTML doesn't mean you should for your new website. The structure and

175

features of a CMS are going to be very important someday. Trust me.

3. **Get some links to your website.** If you have a personal website, link to it from there. If you have investors, they're likely more than happy to link to your new website (if they aren't already). The goal is to get the Google crawler to start indexing your site and start building some authority and trust for your website domain. To check whether your site is being indexed by Google, do a search such as site:yoursite.com (not perfect, but good enough).

4. **Set up a Twitter account.** The name of the account should match your company/domain name. Link to your Twitter account from your main site and to your main site from your Twitter account. (Note: If you have a natural skepticism of the value of Twitter, you are welcome to this skepticism. But go ahead and grab your Twitter account name anyway. You can resume your skepticism after you do that.)

5. **Set up an e-mail subscription.** Although we're big fans of RSS, and we wish the rest of the world were too, not everyone is there yet. Allow your website visitors to be notified of updates by e-mail.

6. **Get a nice logo.** Don't obsess over it, and don't spend thousands of dollars on it. You can run a quick contest on 99designs or CrowdSpring, or find a freelance designer on the web or through your network. Make sure you get the vector file (Illustrator or EPS file) as part of the final deliverable. Logos are pretty important online, because you'll be using a variation of it for many of your online profiles. Quick tips on logos: Simple is better, because simple is more flexible. You're going to use the logo in a variety of ways. In print, online, and maybe even on marketing giveaways.

7. **Set up a simple Facebook business page.** This is also known as a "fan" page. You're not going to get many fans in the early days. That's OK. Just get something out there. Add a simple description of your business and link back to your main website.

8. **Create a simple Facebook URL.** Facebook now allows specifying a custom URL for your fan page. So, you can create

something like http://facebook.com/hubspot (instead of the ugly URL Facebook gives you by default). Take advantage of this feature. For bonus points, set up a sub-domain and re-direct it to your Facebook page. For example, here's what we did: facebook.hubspot.com. Setting up this sub-domain is free and usually pretty easy (it's done through the registrar for your domain).

9. **Kick off a blog.** You can use one of the free hosting tools (like WordPress.com), but *don't* use their domain name. Put your blog on blog.yourcompany.com, or if you have the technical proficiency, make it yourcompany.com/blog. Do NOT make it yourcompany.wordpress.com because you want to control all the SEO authority for your blog and channel it towards your main website. Chances are, WordPress.com doesn't need your help with their SEO.

10. **Write a blog article.** Talk about what you're passionate about. What makes your business different? Why did you start it? Describe your favorite customers. Just make yourself write. If writing doesn't come easily to you, it might be difficult at first—but it gets easier.

11. **Set up Google Alerts.** You want to create alerts for at least the following: your company name, link:yourdomain.com, and "industry term." Try to find a good balance for your industry term so you don't get flooded with alerts that you simply will start ignoring. This may take some iteration and refining. (Oh, and use the "As It Happens" option in Google Alerts so you're not waiting around for new alerts to show up.)

12. **Set up SiteAlerts.** This is a new tool that Dharmesh built (because he wanted it for himself). It's like Google Alerts, but tracks many more things than just mentions on the Internet. It's a great way to track and learn from your competitors too (http://SiteAlerts.com).

13. **Find your closest three competitors.** Pretend someone is paying you $10,000 for locating each competitor. Really try hard. Barely managed to find three? Take a lot of effort? Great. Now find three more. Of these six, pick the two that you think have the most marketing savvy. They should have a website Grade > 90, a blog with some readers, a website that you can

envision people using, a Twitter account that they actually post to, and so on. These are the competitors you're going to start tracking and learning from. Add their names and websites to your Google Alerts and SiteAlerts.

14. **Update your LinkedIn profile.** You do have a LinkedIn profile, right? Mention your new startup website, and add a link to your startup to one of the three slots for this purpose. Make sure you specify the anchor text. Don't go with the default of "My Website." The anchor text should be your startup's name and maybe a couple of words describing what it does.

15. **Find relevant Twitter users.** Use the Twitter search feature to find high-impact Twitter users in your industry. Start following them. You want to start forging relationships and building your Twitter network. Resist the temptation to mass-follow a bunch of random people or play other games just to get your follower count up. That's not going to matter. Get some high-quality relationships going.

16. **Create a StumbleUpon account.** Specify your areas of interest (part of the registration). Spend 10 minutes a day (no more!) stumbling and voting things up/down. Start befriending those who are submitting sites that are relevant and interesting for your startup. Don't submit your own stuff—just start contributing.

17. **Find the bloggers who are writing about your topic area.** Subscribe to their feeds, and read their stuff regularly. Leave valuable comments and participate in the conversation. (Do not spam them or write "fluff" comments. If you don't have something useful to add to the conversation, don't comment.)

18. **Start building some business contacts on Facebook.** Organize your users into groups—one for your business and another for friends/family. This will come in handy later. Don't spam people and ask them to visit your website. At this point, your website is still probably not worth visiting.

19. **Grade your website on Website Grader.** Fix the basic errors it finds. You should be able to get a 50+ just by doing the simple things it suggests. Your goal within the first six months is to get to 80+.

20. **Install web analytics software.** You need to start tracking your website traffic. Where is it coming from? Where is it

going? What keywords are pulling in qualified leads? The most popular option here is Google Analytics (which is free).

21. **Engage your blog commenters.** When you start seeing blog comments (it will take time, but you will), make sure to engage them. Leave a comment yourself to continue the conversation, or answer a question that someone had. This demonstrates that you care about the conversation.

22. **Promote your promoters.** When someone links to you or writes about you on his or her blog, help get *him or her* more traffic. Tweet about it. Stumble it. Digg it. Helping others helps you. Further, other people *notice* this behavior and are more likely to link to you and write about you because they know you're not the type to hoard Internet mojo.

23. **Grab your company name on YouTube.** Just like grabbing a domain name and a Twitter account, a YouTube username allows you to post videos and strengthen your brand (e.g., http://youtube.com/hubspot).

24. **Create and post a video or screencast.** A screencast is a simple recording of your computer screen and audio. Record a simple and short "how-to" for something related to your industry. Demonstrate how to do something simple (just because it's simple to you, doesn't mean everyone knows how to do it). Post this video to the YouTube account for your business. Write a blog article with some explanatory material, and embed this video in the article.

25. **Make a list of all the top people in your industry.** Convert this into a blog post. Example: "17 Real Estate Rockstars I'd Love to Have Coffee With." Just list the people and why you think they're great. Link to their websites or online profiles (this is good, because it helps those that read your article and it increases the chances that the people you mention will notice your article and visit).

26. **Subscribe to your personal LinkedIn RSS feed.** It's helpful to keep up with your network of connections and do a quick scan of what's going on with them (who they connect to, which groups they join, etc.). The best way to do this is to subscribe to your personal RSS feed. To do this, click on the orange RSS icon in the "Network Updates" section of your home page on LinkedIn.

18 Simple Tips for Naming a New Company

Naming a company is hard. Very hard. Even harder than naming a child, because not only do you have to come up with something that "fits," you have to be relatively original.

On the one hand, the pragmatic entrepreneur thinks: "I shouldn't be wasting time on this—for every successful company with a great name, there's one with a crappy name that did just fine. It doesn't seem like a name has much influence on the outcome at all. I'm going to get back to building the business." I sort of agree with this. You shouldn't obsess about your name. But, you also shouldn't dismiss it as unimportant. Part of the game in growing a company is to try and remove unnecessary friction to your growth. Sure, you could build a spectacularly successful company despite having a lousy name—but why not stack the odds in your favor?

One more reason why spending calories on picking a great name is important: *It's a one-time cost to get a great name—but the benefit is forever*. Conversely, if you short-change this and dismiss it completely, you're going to incur what I'd call "branding debt." Not bad at first, and maybe not a big deal for you ever, but every year, as you grow, you'll have this small voice nagging inside your head saying "Should I change the name of the company?" It's going to be annoying. And the longer you wait, the more expensive the decision is, and the less likely you are to do it. Save yourself some of that future pain, and invest early in picking a decent name. You may still get it wrong, but at least you'll know you *tried*.

So, here are some simple tips and suggestions for naming a new company. Not all of these are weighted equally. And, remember that these are suggestions, not laws.

1. **Make sure it's legal!** This should be obvious, but it's an important step that too many entrepreneurs skip. Before falling in love with a name, make sure that someone else doesn't already have claim to it by way of a trademark. In the United States, you should take a quick peek at http://uspto .gov. The good news is that if you satisfy some of the other conditions mentioned (domain name, Twitter handle, Facebook name), odds are relatively low that someone's already using the name.

2. **Hint at what you do.** You have two paths to go when picking a startup name. You can pick a name that is "synthetic" and made-up (example: Wufoo or Quora) or you can use something that is somewhat descriptive of what you do (example: Backupify or Dropbox). I lean a bit towards the descriptive side of the spectrum—but there are tradeoffs. A lot depends on what you're building. Synthetic names are often great in the long, long-term (easily trademarkable, and you can truly "own" them and infuse them with meaning)—but most of the time, I'm more worried about surviving in the short-term. So, I like simple names that convey a bit of what the company actually does or stands for.

3. **Make it easy to remember.** How do you know whether a startup name is easy to remember? You don't know. So, *test it*. Talk to people. Describe the company. At the end of a 2- to 10-minute conversation, casually ask them if they remember what the name of the company is. If it didn't "register" it's not a failure on their part (and make sure to tell them that), but a failure on your part for not having something that's memorable enough.

4. **Make it unambiguous when spoken.** A quick way to test this is to ask friends and family what they think of the name *over the phone*—and ask them to spell it back to you. If a decent percentage of them get it wrong—or are uncertain, you've got a problem.

5. **Make it unambiguous in Google.** Many of the tricks of the trade you'll use to monitor conversations that mention your company on the web will involve doing some sort of search. If your name is something like "Pumpkin," you're going to have a harder time distinguishing when people are talking about the generic term, or when they're talking about your company.

6. **Start early in the alphabet.** In the pre-Google world, this was done so that you'd show up earlier in lists of things that are often sorted alphabetically (like when you win an award or your name is in the phonebook). In the post-Google world, a similar rationale applies, but what's more important is the position of *links* to your website when it shows up in a list of

things (like a directory). If possible, you want to be in the first page of a multipage article that mentions a bunch of companies. The first page of a multipage directory usually passes more SEO authority to your website than subsequent pages.

7. **The ".com" has to be "gettable."** By "gettable," I mean that it is either not registered yet, or it is available for purchase at a price you're willing to pay. Don't play tricks with the domain name either, like including hyphens. Also, stay away from clever domain names like del.icio.us. The reason is simple: It's not natural for people to type domains that way. (Note: Even del.icio.us eventually switched to the much easier domain, delicious.com.)

8. **The Twitter handle has to be available.** No tricks with numbers and underscores and stuff. You want the most natural, obvious twitter handle that matches your company name. This is not quite as hard as .com domain names—but it's getting harder every day.

9. **The Facebook page should be available.** To test this, try visiting http://facebook.com/yourname and see if there's something there. Or, do a search on Facebook and see what you find.

10. **Keep it short.** Always good advice, but particularly true in the age of Twitter. The more characters in your company name, the more characters in the tweets that people write that mention your company name. The more characters your company name uses up, the less you can actually *say* in a tweet. Generally, try to stay 10 characters or under. Also, the number of characters is not the only consideration—it should be short when spoken as well (that is, have fewer syllables). The fewer the syllables, the easier it is for people to say. Great examples of one- and two-syllable names: Dropbox, Mint, FreshBooks, ZenDesk. I'd shy away from anything that is four or more syllables.

11. **Don't leave out vowels or add punctuation.** Just because Flickr was successful does not mean it's okay for you to drop vowels from your name. Name your company in whatever way is natural—for humans. And, don't add punctuation (like an exclamation mark) to your name.

12. **Try to get your main keyword into the name.** This helps with SEO *and* signals to potential visitors what they might find on your site.

13. **Start with an uppercase letter.** If it's good enough for Google, Amazon, and a thousand other really successful companies, it's good enough for you. Sure, starting with a lowercase letter is cute and might demonstrate some humility, but 99 percent of the people are going to spell it wrong and you're going to spend too many cycles worrying about training them—and you're still going to fail. If you're going to ask the world a favor, save it for the big stuff—not "can you please be sure to spell our company name with a lowercase letter."

14. **Don't name your company after yourself.** Yes, I know it's tempting because it's so *easy*. And, you might even think "hey, customers should know who they're doing business with." You might even make an argument like "there have been plenty of successful startups that were named after their founders." Though that might all be true, on average, this is a losing approach. When customers hear something like "Dharmesh Shah Enterprises" (granted, your name is probably not as odd as mine), it doesn't make them immediately think: "Wow, that must be an awfully cool/successful/stable company." It sounds a bit amateurish right at the get go. The other reason is that if you name the company after yourself, too many people are going to want to talk to *you*. That's okay when you're the only person in the company to talk to, but it becomes problematic as your company grows and there are other people trying to sell/support/market.

15. **Don't use an acronym.** These were all the rage at various points in time—but I'm not a big fan. It's hard to get emotional about a three-letter acronym. It's hard to hug an acronym. As a corollary to this, try not to have a company name with three words in it, because it's long enough that people are going to be tempted to reduce it to an acronym.

16. **Have a story.** When someone asks (and they will), "so why did you pick *X* for your name?", it's nice to have something relatively interesting to say. Names are a part of your personality, and the absence of a personality is rarely a good thing.

For example, when I started my first company (I was 24 and didn't know what branding was), the name I picked violated many of the rules in this list. The company name was "Pyramid Digital Solutions." But, it had a pretty good back story. I started first with the acronym P.D.S. I wanted to name the company after my dad (whose initials are PDS). He's a tad superstitious and didn't want me to name the company after him (it's a long story). And, wanting to prove him wrong (as children are often inclined to do), I started with the acronym PDS.

17. **Pay attention to character sequences in multiword names.** This one's a bit subtle. But, if you have a name that is two words stuck together, be mindful of what character ends the first word, and what starts the second. I'd stay away from names where both of those letters are the same. Example: If your company name is something like BetterReading, it's suboptimal (because better ends with "R" and reading starts with "R." Normally, that's okay, but when you type it out as a URL, people will often see: betterreading.com—which is not terrible, but does cause the brain to "pause" for a microsecond because it feels a tad unnatural. And, I'd be remiss if I didn't bring up the widely popular example of unfortunate character sequences expertsexchange.com. When capitalized properly, this name is just fine (ExpertsExchange), which is what the site owners intended. But, it turns out, this can be confused as "ExpertSexChange" (which is not what was intended). Make sure you think through the combinations properly.

18. **Seek timeless instead of trendy.** It seems that every generation of startups has their own "trendy" approach to names. Examples are the dropping-vowels thing (like Flickr), the breaking up of words (like del.icio.us), or the newly fashionable ".ly" and ".io" names. Give your company a timeless name that will still work many years from now.

Insider Tips on Buying the Domain Name You Love

Chances are, as you try to think of a great domain name for your company, you're going to quickly encounter how formidable of a task this is. Every English word, and even combinations of English words are all taken. You could spend hours trying to come up with a name that is not taken yet—and still not come up with anything. So, you consider resorting to tricky things like dropping vowels from the name you want, or misspelling it in some weird way. This is suboptimal.

Though it is indeed difficult to find great domain names that are just available "free and clear," it is still possible to purchase a domain name with a reasonable budget.

Here are some notes on domain names—how to look for them and how to buy them.

1. The first step is making a list of domain names that you think would be acceptable. A common mistake people make is trying one domain at a time, getting excited when they see that there's no website on the domain, and then getting disappointed when they can't register it. Then, they move on to the next one, and the next one. This is an inefficient process.

2. It's important to recognize that just because you visit the domain name and there is no website that does *not* mean that the domain name is available. Domain names can (and are) registered without any website hosted on them.

3. To determine whether a domain is registered, you'll need to use a "whois" tool. There are many options out there (most are free). I prefer using http://DomainTools.com, which is reliable and provides information about when the domain was registered, and who the domain is registered to.

4. The best way I've found to come up with a suitable domain name is to make a list of words that describe the business or are attributes that I might consider appropriate. Then, you can combine these words to see if a particular combination of words is unique enough whereby the domain is available free and clear.

    My favorite tool for this is: http://instantdomainsearch.com. It's a quick way to test the availability of a domain (though it's not always completely accurate).

5. When searching for domain names, you may come across domains that are available for premium purchase. That's usually good news (as long as the price is something within your

budget). In this case, the domain is being sold through one of the large domain resellers, and conducting a transaction is relatively straightforward. You negotiate a price, and use an escrow service to channel the funds through a third party. Once the domain is in your possession, the escrow agent releases the funds to the seller.

6. The toughest situation is when you fall in love with a specific domain but have no idea as to whether the current owner is willing to sell it, and for what price. Here are the quick steps I would take in this case:

   a. Determine who owns the domain using http://Domain Tools.com

   b. Make contact (via e-mail) with the domain owner. This is an important e-mail. Remember the *goal* of this initial e-mail is to get a response. If you make the rookie move of saying "I'm interested in your domain name, would you like to sell it . . ." there's a decent chance that you will hear *no* response from the seller. If you want to maximize your chances for a response, you need to do a few things: (1) Make sure that you make a reasonable offer for the domain and *put that offer in the e-mail.* (2) Make clear that should you come to an agreeable price, you will immediately place the funds into escrow, pending transfer of the domain. (3) Let the seller know that you are considering several possible domain names—and you'll be making a decision quickly—but his or her domain fits the project the best, so it is your preference.

Get Inbound Certified!

Join the Best and Brightest Marketers from Around the World and Earn Your Inbound Certification

HubSpot Academy's Inbound Certification covers the spectrum of what inbound is all about, starting with big picture concepts and delving deep into tried and true tactics. From the essentials of an effective inbound strategy to crafting remarkable landing pages to becoming a guru at segmentation, this certification will help you master every stage of the Inbound Methodology.

Whether you're a student or a seasoned marketer, the Inbound Certification will provide the know-how to help you better attract strangers, convert visitors, close leads, and delight customers.

Visit academy.hubspot.com/certification to learn more about which Inbound Certification is right for you.

Index

Praise for *Inbound Marketing*

"Halligan and Shah are on the frontlines of discovering and systemizing marketing methods that will be the standard soon enough. Jump the line and learn about inbound marketing today. This book is the beginning."
—Chris Brogan
Author of *The Freaks Shall Inherit the Earth*

"You don't need a degree from MIT to figure out inbound marketing. This book makes it simple and approachable."
—Ed Roberts
Founder and Chair,
MIT Entrepreneurship Center

"As *Inbound Marketing* so eloquently explains, there's no black magic to successfully attracting customers via the web. Read this book, apply its lessons. It works."
—Rand Fishkin
Moz

"If you've been looking for a trustworthy primer on getting found online, here's a great place to start. Buy one for your clueless colleague too."
—Seth Godin
Author of *Meatball Sundae*

"I wish I'd had a book like *Inbound Marketing* when I first started out online. This is the roadmap every small business needs for online marketing success today."
—Anita Campbell
Editor in Chief, SmallBizTrends.com

"If you have more money than brains, you should focus on outbound marketing. If you have more brains than money, you should focus on inbound marketing by reading this book."
—Guy Kawasaki
Cofounder of Alltop, and author of *Reality Check*